The Official Guide to
THE
Print Shop Deluxe Ensemble II

The Official Guide to
THE
Print Shop® Deluxe
Ensemble™ II

James R. Caruso and Mavis E. Arthur

SYBEX®

San Francisco ◆ Paris ◆ Düsseldorf ◆ Soest

Acquisitions Manager: Kristine Plachy
Developmental Editor: Damon Dean
Editor: Valerie Potter
Technical Editor: Maurie Duggan
Desktop Publisher: Alissa Feinberg
Production Coordinator: Renée Avalos
Book Designer: Suzanne Albertson
Technical Artist: Guy Michel
Indexer: Linda Facey
Cover Designer: Joanna Gladden
Comic characters designed by Llorenç Amer Catà. Copyright ©1993, ARTimatge S.A.

The chapter heads were designed and created using The Print Shop® Deluxe Ensemble™ II by the authors, James R. Caruso and Mavis E. Arthur.

Library of Congress Card Number: 95-72473

ISBN: 0-7821-1816-X

Manufactured in the United States of America

10 9 8 7 6 5 4 3 2 1

We'd like to dedicate this book to the developers of this incredibly versatile and imaginative program that makes artists of us all—the Brøderbund team.

Acknowledgments

This book was written with the assistance of a really super team in the marketing, public relations, customer service, and product management departments at Brøderbund Software, Inc. They not only provided us with anything we needed to make a great book but also assisted in making this the *official* book on Print Shop Deluxe Ensemble II. For all their help and confidence, we are grateful.

We'd also like to thank the team at Sybex who helped us to pull it all together and make it work, including Damon Dean, developmental editor; Valerie Potter, editor; Maurie Duggan, technical editor; Alissa Feinberg, desktop publisher; Renée Avalos, production coordinator; Guy Michel, technical artist; and Linda Facey, indexer.

And last, we'd like to thank Jane Reh, who helped to make it happen.

Contents at a Glance

Introduction   xxi

Part One: The Beginning   1

1   Creating Your First Project   3

2   Discovering Tools   29

3   Mastering Menus   55

4   Getting Help   89

5   Understanding Print Shop Projects   101

Part Two: Managing Graphics   123

6   Working with Graphics Libraries   125

7   Creating Special Graphics   143

8   Importing Images   165

9   Exporting Graphics   175

Part Three: Finishing Touches   185

10   Working with Text and Headlines   187

11   Creating and Merging Lists   213

12   Printing Made Easy   231

Appendices   239

A   Installing Print Shop Deluxe Ensemble II   241

B   A Compilation of Notes   245

C   Specialized Paper Sources   261

Index   265

Table of Contents

Introduction

xxi

Part One: The Beginning
1

◆

Chapter 1:
Creating Your First Project

3

Making a Project Decision	4
Starting a Project	4
Choosing a Method	4
Choosing an Orientation	6
Designing the Front of the Card	7
Selecting a Backdrop	7
Selecting a Layout	11
Creating a Headline	13
Editing Text	15
Moving Objects	18
Adding a Graphic	18
Designing the Inside of the Card	21
Selecting a Backdrop	21
Selecting a Layout	22
Adding Text	24
Designing the Back of the Card	24
Selecting a Graphic	25
Putting a Frame around the Text Box	25
Endnotes	26

Chapter 2:
Discovering Tools

29

Starting the Project   30
Getting Acquainted with the Toolbar   32
Moving and Resizing Objects   33
   Moving a Single Object   33
   Moving Multiple Objects Together 34
   Resizing Graphics   35
   Resizing Headline or Text Blocks 36
Rotating Objects   38
   Rotating a Single Object   38
   Rotating Multiple Objects Together 39
Moving Around in the Document   40
Adding Objects   42
   Understanding Placeholders   42
   Adding Objects with Placeholders 44
   Customizing Placeholders   45
Changing the View   46
Deleting Objects   47
Flipping Objects   48
Framing Objects   48
Undoing or Redoing Your Last Action   50
   Undoing Your Last Action   50
   Redoing Your Last Action   50
Coloring and Shading an Area   51
Endnotes   54

Chapter 3:
Mastering Menus

55

Using the File Menu   56
   Starting a New Project   56
   Opening an Existing File   57

Saving a File   58
Saving As   60
Reverting to a Previously Saved Version   61
Choosing Preferences   61
Printing a Project   63
Setting Up Your Printer   64
Previewing a Project   64
Exiting the Program   65
Using the Edit Menu   65
Undoing an Action   65
Cutting Objects   66
Copying Objects   67
Pasting Objects   67
Deleting Objects   68
Duplicating Objects   68
Selecting All   69
Using the Object Menu   70
Adding Objects   70
Editing Objects   70
Adding Shadows to Objects   74
Framing an Object   75
Putting Objects in Order   75
Scaling an Object   76
Rotating an Object   77
Flipping Objects   78
Locking and Unlocking Objects   78
Aligning Objects   79
Using the Project Menu   80
Changing the Backdrop   80
Changing the Layout   81
Changing the Banner Length   82
Blending the Colors on a Page   84
Choosing Other Project Commands   86
Using the View Menu   86
Using the Extras Menu   86
Using Smart Graphics   87
Customizing Libraries   87

Accessing Lists   87
Exporting Graphics   87
Using the Help Menu   88
Endnotes   88

Chapter 4:

Getting Help

89

Using the Main Help Screen   89
Using Links   91
Using the Help Chapters   92
Using Keyboard Shortcuts   92
Searching Help   93
Using the Help Menu Bar   95
Using the File Menu   95
Using the Edit Menu   96
Using the Topics Menu   98
Using the Help Menu   98
Accessing the Using Help Library   98
Finding Help in Dialog Boxes   99
Endnotes   100

Chapter 5:

Understanding Print Shop Projects

101

Common Design Elements   102
Selecting a Path   102
Choosing an Orientation   103
Browsing for a Backdrop   104
Selecting a Layout   105
Project-Specific Design Elements   106
Designing Greeting Cards   107

Designing Signs and Posters   108
Designing Banners   110
Designing Certificates   112
Designing Stationery   114
Designing Calendars   116
Designing Labels   119
One Last Tip   121
Endnotes   122

Part Two: Managing Graphics
123

Chapter 6:
Working with Graphics Libraries

125

Types of Graphics   126
Navigating the Graphics Browser   127
Starting a Project   128
Broadening the Search Options   129
Searching by Category   130
Searching by Multiple Keywords   130
Searching with Project Text   133
Merging Graphics Libraries   134
Preparing to Merge Libraries   135
Starting the Merge   137
Modifying Graphics Libraries   138
Preparing to Modify a Library   138
Modifying a Library   139
Endnotes   141

Chapter 7:
Creating Special Graphics

143

Customizing Smart Graphics	144
Designing an Initial Cap	145
Designing a Number	150
Selecting a Timepiece	152
Naming Smart Graphics	154
Customizing Borders	154
Arranging a Border	155
Choosing Border Graphics	157
Saving a Custom Border	159
Adding a Custom Border to a Project	160
Designing a Seal	160
Adding a Graphic	160
Adding Text	162
Saving a Customized Seal	163
Endnotes	164

Chapter 8:
Importing Images

165

Importing Graphics	166
Choosing a Graphic Format	166
Looking at Available Files	168
Importing a Graphic	168
An Importing Tip	169
Importing Photos	169
Cropping Photos	172
Resizing Photos	173
Endnotes	173

Chapter 9:
Exporting Graphics
175

Opening the Graphics Exporter   176
Choosing a Graphic   176
Exporting a Graphic   178
   Designating a File Type   178
   Choosing a Destination   180
Exporting a Library   180
   Printing a Catalog   181
   Printing to File   182
   Exiting the Graphics Exporter 183
Endnotes   183

Part Three: Finishing Touches
185

◆

Chapter 10:
Working with Text and Headlines
187

Editing Text Blocks   188
   Choosing Text Attributes   189
   Using the Text Bar   191
Working with Headlines   193
   Changing Headline Text Attributes   195
   Choosing a Headline Shape   196
   Customizing Headline Text   197
Working with Title Blocks   200
   Choosing Type Styles for Title Blocks 200
   Customizing a Title   200

Adding a Signature Block   201
  Selecting a Block Type   202
  Choosing Text Attributes for Signature Lines   202
  Adding Text to Signature Blocks   204
  Inserting Autographs   204
Adding a Word Balloon   206
Exploring Quotes and Verses   209
Endnotes   212

Chapter 11:
Creating and Merging Lists

213

Creating Lists   214
  Making an Address List   214
  Making a Custom List   218
Modifying Lists   220
Merging Lists   221
  Merging a List into a Project   222
  Choosing a List to Merge   223
  Selecting Merge Fields   224
Printing a List   226
Importing Lists   228
Exporting Lists   228
Endnotes   229

Chapter 12:
Printing Made Easy

231

Printing Specific Projects   232
  Printing Banners   232
  Printing Name Lists   233
  Printing Labels   233

Printing Business Cards   234
Printing Envelopes   235
Troubleshooting Print Problems   236
Dealing with Partial Printouts   236
Printing TrueType Fonts   237
Endnotes   237

Appendices
239

◆

Appendix A:
Installing Print Shop Deluxe Ensemble II
241

Starting the Installation   241
Program Installation   242
Starting the Program   243

Appendix B:
A Compilation of Notes
245

Chapter 1: Creating Your First Project   245
Starting a Project   245
Designing the Front of the Card   246
Chapter 2: Discovering Tools   247
Starting the Project   247
Moving and Resizing Objects   247
Moving Around in the Document   248
Deleting Objects   248
Framing Objects   248
Undoing or Redoing Your Last Action   248
Coloring and Shading an Area   249

Chapter 3: Mastering Menus ... 249
  Using the Edit Menu ... 249
  Using the Object Menu ... 249
  Using the Project Menu ... 250
Chapter 4: Getting Help ... 250
  Using the Main Help Screen ... 250
  Using the Help Menu Bar ... 251
Chapter 5: Understanding Print Shop Projects ... 251
  Project-Specific Design Elements ... 251
Chapter 6: Working with Graphics Libraries ... 252
  Types of Graphics ... 252
  Navigating the Graphics Browser ... 252
  Merging Graphics Libraries ... 253
  Modifying Graphics Libraries ... 253
Chapter 7: Creating Special Graphics ... 254
  Customizing Smart Graphics ... 254
  Designing a Seal ... 255
Chapter 8: Importing Images ... 255
  Importing Graphics ... 255
Chapter 9: Exporting Graphics ... 256
  Choosing a Graphic ... 256
  Exporting a Graphic ... 256
  Exporting a Library ... 257
Chapter 10: Working with Text and Headlines ... 257
  Editing Text Blocks ... 257
  Working with Headlines ... 258
  Working with Title Blocks ... 258
  Adding a Word Balloon ... 258
  Exploring Quotes and Verses ... 259
Chapter 11: Creating and Merging Lists ... 259
  Creating Lists ... 259
  Merging Lists ... 260
  Printing a List ... 260
Chapter 12: Printing Made Easy ... 260
  Printing Specific Projects ... 260

Appendix C:
Specialized Paper Sources

261

Avery®	261
Beaver Prints™	261
Idea Art	262
Paper Access	262
Paper Direct®	262
Queblo®	263

Index

265

Introduction

You are in for a treat. You now own the latest version of the number one personal publishing software. With more than seven million copies sold, Brøderbund's Print Shop is without question the standard for graphics programs, letting you create a variety of projects with ease. Not only that, it's fun.

This newest version, called Print Shop Deluxe Ensemble II, is designed to perform under Microsoft Windows 3.1 or Windows 95, and it takes giant steps in making it even easier to create striking projects. It keeps all the exciting features of past programs and adds:

◆ The Graphics Browser

◆ Hundreds of ready-to-print designs

◆ Hundreds of pre-written greetings, quotes, and verses

◆ Accessibility to all projects from one main screen

◆ More than 4,500 graphics

◆ Printable Help and graphics catalogs

In addition to all of the above, you have at your fingertips 73 TrueType fonts and 3,500 combinations of text styles and shapes. In other words, you have nearly unlimited creative possibilities.

What was great just got better with the release of Print Shop Deluxe Ensemble II.

Your mission is to learn how to make use of every feature. This book endeavors to help you accomplish your mission and to push this program to its limits.

◆ Features of the Book

This book is designed as both a reference tool and as a hands-on guide, taking you step by step through the process of creating projects with Print Shop Deluxe Ensemble II using the following features:

Mission Every chapter begins with a mission, an objective for that particular chapter to keep you motivated and informed about what lies ahead.

Visuals This book is full of illustrations, designed to make the reading simpler and the understanding more comprehensive. Print Shop is a graphics-intensive program. You'll see the creative use of a great many Print Shop graphics within the pages of this book.

Hands-On Exercises Chapter 1 sets the tone for the book by jump-starting you right into a project, involving you from the very beginning in the creation process with this versatile and interesting program. As you move from chapter to chapter, you'll be propelled through the features that make this program truly outstanding as a creative tool. Every chapter will involve you, enveloping you in the intricacies and nuances of the program while putting you in control of your own understanding.

Special Projects You'll have a chance to work creatively with ready-made projects as well as design a few new ones. You'll be encouraged to strike out on your own, to infuse your own ingenuity into the projects that fill these pages.

 Special notes call your attention to tips that might be helpful or to information that will save you time and frustration in the creative process.

Endnotes Every chapter ends with a wrap-up of what was covered in the chapter, followed by a preview of what lies ahead in the next chapter.

◆ Structure of the Book

This book is divided into three parts:

Part One: The Beginning This part of the book gets you started on your first project and introduces you to the basics of the toolbar, the main menu, and the Help system. Finally, it takes you on a tour of the individual Print Shop projects.

Part Two: Managing Graphics Your Print Shop graphics library has more than 4,500 graphics—and that's before you add your own. That's great, but with so many, how do you remember what's there, and how do you find them when you want to use them? This part of the book will give you tips on searching graphic libraries and suggest ways to analyze the structure and content of the graphics libraries so you can customize them to suit your own areas of interest.

Part Three: Finishing Touches Now that you know your way around Print Shop and you can manage all the graphics you'll ever need, this part of the book covers the final details of creating a project, such as working with text, creating and merging lists, and solving printing problems. (The importance of this last topic can't be overestimated: you may have the greatest project in the world, but if you can't print it out, who will know?)

Additionally, there are three appendices in this book. Appendix A tells you how to install PSD Ensemble II on both Windows 3.1 and Windows 95. Appendix B provides a recap of all the notes in the book, cross-referenced by chapter and heading. Browse through this appendix and when you see a note that intrigues you, go to that section of the book and read the accompanying procedure. Finally, Appendix C tells you where to find special paper on which to print your perfect project.

In short, this book is designed to be not only instructive but also fun. We had fun writing it. We hope you'll have as much fun using it to learn everything there is to know about Print Shop Deluxe Ensemble II.

◆ Off You Go

While it is true that you will be able to create a good project without learning the finer points of Print Shop, it's equally true that you will be able to create a really terrific project if you take the extra time to learn what the program can do and how far you can push it with your own creativity. The frustration factor will be much lower if you spend the time now to run through the basics of how the program operates, what it has to offer, and how you can make all this work for you and your projects.

You're about to take a journey through a truly exciting program. Enjoy the ride!

Part One:

The Beginning

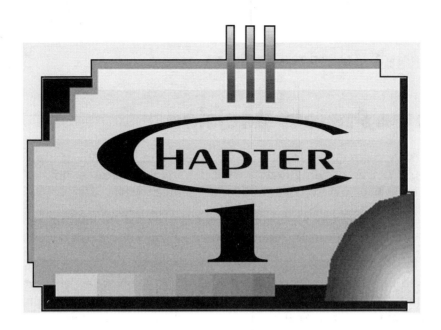

Creating Your First Project

Your mission: to create a Print Shop project

◆

Being creative with Print Shop Deluxe Ensemble II is, as they say, a piece of cake. The program gives you a multitude of choices each step of the way. No matter what the project—greeting card, sign, poster, banner, letterhead, calendar, label, certificate, business card, envelope, or post-card—your final product will truly be your own.

In this chapter, we'll go step-by-step through the process of creating a project with Print Shop. When you finish, you'll know the basics of working with Print Shop, enough to convince you of its versatility and your own ability to create unique projects. So let's make Print Shop do something that we can see and feel, and let's do it in a matter of minutes.

◆ Making a Project Decision

First, a step required in all creative projects and yet the most likely to be skipped over: deciding exactly what is going to be created, not just what it looks like but also what purpose it's going to serve.

Here's the scenario: we're going on a cruise, and we're inviting our friends to join us for a shipboard party—a Bon Voyage party—right before we depart. So we need an invitation to the party.

With the help of our computer, Print Shop, and you, we are going to make an original invitation, one that will not only please us but tell our friends all about the party. We'll want to include the following information:

◆ When the party is

◆ Where the party is

◆ What kind of party it's going to be

◆ Starting a Project

With all that in mind, let's start.

1. If you haven't started the program yet, double-click on the Print Shop icon to open the program.

The first screen that you see is the program title, followed quickly by the Select a Project dialog box. As you can see in Figure 1.1, your project choices are Greeting Cards, Signs & Posters, Banners, Certificates, Stationery, Calendars, Labels, and Extras.

2. Click on Greeting Cards.

Choosing a Method

The Select a Path dialog box appears. Here you can choose between using a ready-made card or starting from scratch. Ready-made cards are just

that, cards that are ready to print or customize. They can be useful, but for this project we want to design our own.

3. Click on Start From Scratch.

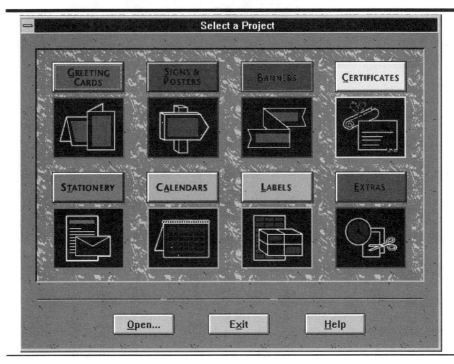

Figure 1.1: Print Shop's Select a Project screen

Choosing an Orientation

Now you're asked to choose a greeting card orientation. Figure 1.2 shows the four different ways you can lay out a greeting card in Print Shop: Side Fold, Side Fold Spread, Top Fold, and Top Fold Spread.

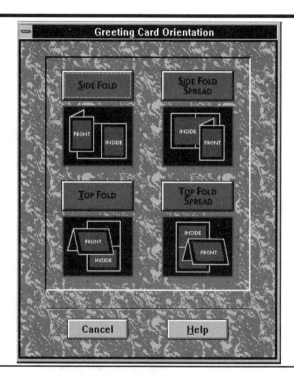

Figure 1.2:   Choose a greeting card orientation.

For our invitation, we'll choose Side Fold Spread, which gives us a front and back page area of 5½" high by 4¼" wide. The inside panel of the card is 5½" high by 8½" wide.

4. Click on Side Fold Spread to select it.

All Greeting Card layouts work with one sheet of 8½" ➤ 11" paper, folded to fit the specific card orientation. The Side Fold selection gives you four panels 5½" high by 4¼" wide, the Top Fold selection gives you four panels 4¼" high by 5½" wide, and the Top Fold Spread gives you a front and back panel 5½" wide by 4¼" high with the inside panel 5½" wide by 8½" high. (The actual printable area for each spread is somewhat smaller.)

◆ Designing the Front of the Card

Once you've chosen the orientation, Print Shop assumes you want to start working on the front of the card right away. The first screen you see is the Backdrops Browser.

 The first thing you'll be asked to design is the front of the greeting card. You'll design the inside and back of the greeting card after you reach the main project window.

Selecting a Backdrop

The Backdrops Browser offers many graphics choices listed by descriptive names. Note that the default library is PSD (Print Shop Deluxe) Backdrops; in this library, you can select from 94 different graphics. The choices offered are names that briefly describe the backdrops.

1. To see what each one looks like, click on the file name once to highlight it, and it will show up in the preview box, as shown in Figure 1.3.

Take some time now to preview some of the fabulous backdrops Print Shop makes available.

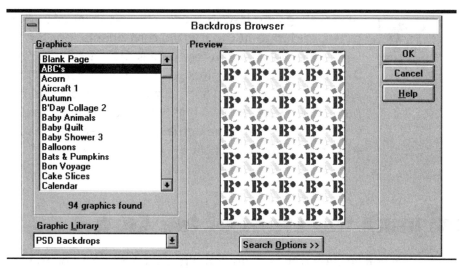

Figure 1.3:   You can preview available backdrops in the Backdrops Browser screen.

Accessing Other Graphics Libraries

Now let's take a look at the other graphics libraries.

2. Click on the arrow that appears next to the Graphic Library box in the lower-left corner (it now says PSD Backdrops). You'll note that you have other libraries available. You can select one of these, or you can select All Libraries and all the graphics will be available.

3. Select All Libraries.

Using Search Options

We now have 144 graphics from which to choose our backdrop. Let's narrow the search a bit.

4. Click on Search Options. The Backdrops Browser dialog box expands and offers options to help you locate a graphic that's perfect for your project (see Figure 1.4).

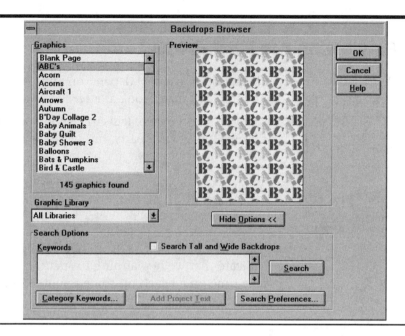

Figure 1.4:   When you click on Search Options, the Backdrops Browser box expands to include an area where you can specify search criteria.

5. Click on Category Keywords. The Select Category Keywords dialog box appears, from which you can choose one or more of 16 different categories.

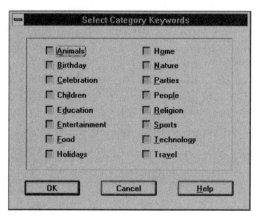

6. Since we're having a party prior to departing on a trip, select Travel, then OK. You return to the Backdrops Browser screen with Travel appearing in the dialog search box.

7. Click the Search button to see what backdrops are available with a travel theme. Eleven backdrop names appear in the graphics list.

8. Click on Hide Options to hide the search options.

Previewing the Backdrops

The decision of which backdrop to use will depend on your own interpretation of the party theme. Let's take a look at a few.

9. Click on Bon Voyage. It seems an obvious choice for our Bon Voyage party, but let's take a look at some others before we make a decision.

10. Click on Coastal Scene. If we selected it, it could indicate that we're planning to spend considerable time on a beach on some remote island. That's a nice idea.

11. Click on Travel, and there we are lounging on the beach with a cruise ship at anchor waiting for our return. We could live with that scenario.

12. Click on Ocean & Jungle for a totally different theme.

13. Click on Picture Postcard and a beach chair awaits our ship's arrival.

As you can see, there are plenty of choices for the backdrop that express diverse party themes and still allow plenty of room for individual creativity. If none of these fit the project, you can choose Blank Page and design your own or import a totally different graphic, as you'll discover in Chapter 8, "Importing Images."

14. For now, let's select the Bon Voyage backdrop. Click on it, then click OK.

Selecting a Layout

The next screen that appears, the Select a Layout dialog box (see Figure 1.5), offers a selection of layout designs. These are designed to help determine where to put the text and graphic elements.

If you choose No Layout, the Bon Voyage graphic will remain as it is. Once you're in the main project window, you can add your own layout elements.

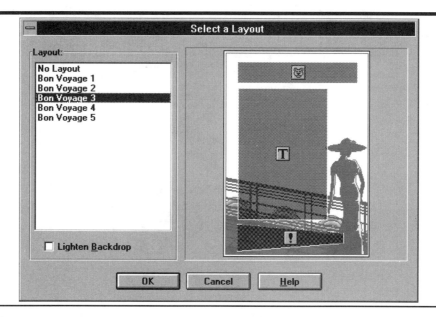

Figure 1.5:   Select a Layout offers a selection of layout designs.

Let's see what the stock layouts look like:

1. Highlight one and then another. Each layout selected is previewed over the backdrop.

The shaded boxes on the layouts are called *placeholders*. They hold a place for type or headlines or graphics. Headline placeholders have an exclamation point (!) on them, text placeholders have a *T*, and graphics placeholders have Print Shop's Smiley Bear icon.

2. For this project, click on Layout 2, then click OK. You move directly to the main project window with the basics of the invitation in place, as shown in Figure 1.6.

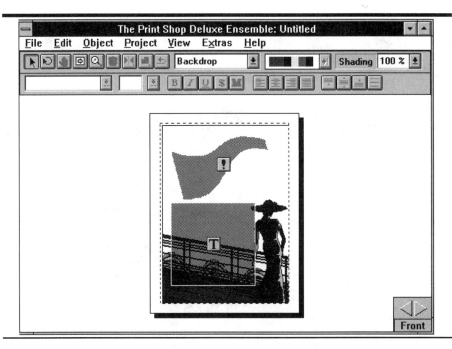

Figure 1.6:   Once you've selected the backdrop and layout for your card, you jump to the main project window, where you can continue designing the project.

Creating a Headline

Now we need to fill in the headline placeholder.

1. Double-click on the exclamation point. You go directly to the Headline dialog box, shown here.

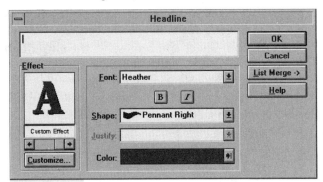

2. The cursor is parked in a blank rectangle in this headline composition screen. Type your title here. In this case, type **WIND SONG**, the name of our cruise ship.

Headline text sizes itself to fit the headline placeholder box. If you want a smaller or larger text type, resize the headline box, and the text will automatically resize to fit the new box.

Changing the Font

Below and to the left of this rectangle is an area labeled Effect. In this area is a capital letter *A* in the selected font style (indicated to the right in a box labeled Font). The font can be changed easily by clicking on the Font box and choosing from the selections offered.

3. Select the font Moderne by highlighting it; the *A* changes to this new type style. This is a good way to check a font to make sure it's the style you want.

4. Under the font selection box are two buttons: one labeled B, to make the type bold, and one labeled I, to italicize the type. Select bold to make the headline stand out more.

Customizing the Text

Now let's look at customizing the headline text. You can customize this text by adding shadow, outlining, or filling with color in a variety of ways. The Print Shop program has already created 25 different combinations of these effects. You can scroll through these by clicking on the Custom Effect slider box under the letter *A*. As you scroll through, you'll note that the effect title changes from Effect 1 to Effect 2 to Effect 3 and so on. The 26th effect is labeled Custom Effect and represents the current effect.

You can create your own custom effect by clicking on the button labeled Customize. The Custom Effect dialog box pops up. Here you can select a text effect, a shadow effect, and the color of your elements.

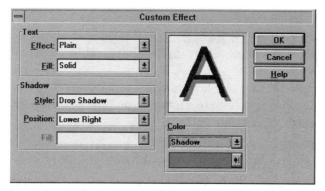

From Text Effect, choose from Plain, Thin Outline, Thick Outline, and Highlighted. From Text Fill, choose from Solid, Blend Across, Blend Down, Radiant, and Double Blend. From Shadow Style, choose from No Shadow, Drop Shadow, Block Shadow, and Silhouette. If you select Drop Shadow or Block Shadow, choose Upper Right, Upper Left, Lower Right, or Lower Left from the Shadow Position box. If you select Silhouette, choose Solid, Blend Across, Blend Down, Radiant, or Double Blend from the Shadow Fill box. From Color, choose what you want to color: Text, Text Blend, Outline, Shadow, or Shadow Blend. And, finally, make your color selection from the color palette.

5. For now, press Cancel to leave this box and go back to the Headline box.

6. Select Effect 13 from the custom effects.

7. Click on Customize and the Custom Effect box returns. Note that Effect 13 is shown as the current effect.

8. Cancel out of Custom Effect and return to Headline.

9. Click OK.

You return to the main window with *WIND SONG*, the name of the ship, now inserted into the headline placeholder on the invitation. You can see what it looks like against the backdrop in Figure 1.7.

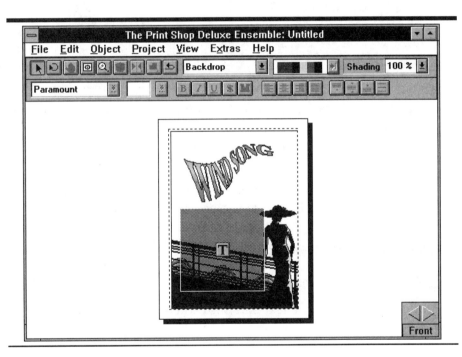

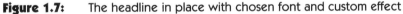

Figure 1.7:   The headline in place with chosen font and custom effect

Editing Text

Next we want to fill the text placeholder to finish off the text on the front of the card.

1. Double-click on the text placeholder.

The Edit Text dialog box, shown here, pops up. This screen offers a variety of options for font type, style, size, and color. You can also choose how you'd like to justify the text in its placeholder. If you're at a loss for

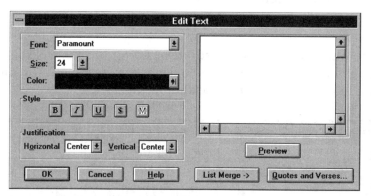

words, you can click on Quotes and Verses to get some ideas. You can also merge a custom list. We'll explore these options in Chapter 10.

2. For our invitation, select Paramount as the font and 30 as the type size.

3. Select bold by clicking on the B and shadow by clicking on the S as style options.

4. Choose Horizontal Center and Vertical Center to center the type in the text block, both side-to-side and top-to-bottom.

Entering the Text

Now let's type the text in the text area.

5. Click once in the text entry box, then type the following:

    A

    Bon

    Voyage

    Party

All finished. Let's take a look at our creation.

6. Click on the Preview button. All of the text selections are shown in the preview window.

Changing the Text Color

Looks great. Let's do one last thing: change the color of the type.

 The Preview button becomes the Edit button when you are in preview mode. If you want to change the text, click on Edit and the text box changes back to normal so you can change or add to the text (the button changes back to Preview at the same time).

7. Click on the Edit button; the type goes back to its original no-style work font.

8. Highlight the type by placing the cursor to the left of the first letter, *A*, holding down the mouse button, and dragging the cursor all the way down through the last letter, *y*. This highlights the complete statement.

9. Click on the arrow next to the Color box and a pop-up palette of color chips appears. If you're working in grayscale rather than color, this pop-up palette will offer you shades of gray rather than color.

10. Select the color or shade you want your type to be. When you release the mouse button, the selected color shows in the color box.

You can now preview the selection as you did before, but in its new color.

11. If all the selections are OK, click on OK and the type will be placed on the front of the invitation. The finished product is shown here.

Moving Objects

Now that you see the front of the invitation all together, you may want to reposition the text or headline blocks. To move an object:

1. First, select it using the Pointer tool. The Pointer, an arrow pointing up and left, is the first button in the toolbar at the top of the main window. Click on the Pointer tool, then click once in the headline area; a box will appear around the words WIND SONG.

 It is important to remember that you must select the object or text with the Pointer tool before you can do anything to it. Menus and tool options will be offered based on what you've selected to edit. If you've selected a graphic, graphic options will be available. If you've selected text, text options will be offered.

2. Place the cursor inside the box, then hold down the left mouse button while you drag the box—and the headline along with it— to what you feel is a better position (toward the top of the page, for instance).

3. Now do the same to the box that appears when you click on the words *A Bon Voyage Party*. Notice that the text box can be moved to any position on the backdrop, or to any place inside the window, for that matter.

You can also make the box larger or smaller by grabbing the *handles* (the square boxes at each corner) and pulling or pushing on them. Handles appear when you select an object with the Pointer tool. We will tell you more about this feature in Chapter 2, "Discovering Tools."

Adding a Graphic

The final element for the front of the invitation is an indication that refreshments will be served. We could just put in another text box and type the words, but it might be more fun and creative to put in a graphic.

1. Click on Object on the menu bar at the top of the window.

2. Click on Add in the menu that drops down; you are offered a choice of graphic shapes that can be added to the invitation.

What we'd like to do is find a graphic of a cold drink or some other refreshment we can place in the bottom-left corner of the invitation. Since most Print Shop graphics are square, let's start with that category.

3. Choose Square Graphic from the list. A placeholder for a square graphic appears in the center of the project as shown here.

4. Double-click on the icon in the center of the graphic and you will be presented with a list of graphics and graphics libraries, shown in Figure 1.8.

By default, the PSD Squares library is listed. There are 277 graphics in this library. Pretty overwhelming. Let's narrow our search.

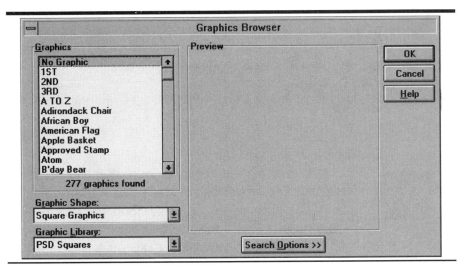

Figure 1.8: When you click on the square graphic placeholder, the Graphics Browser presents you with a variety of options.

5. Click on Search Options, and the Graphics Browser expands to include search criteria just like the Backdrops Browser did.

Once you turn on search options, they will remain open in all subsequent Browser dialog boxes until you hide them.

6. Click on Category Keywords and take a look at the options offered.

Unfortunately, the categories offered do not include drinks or refreshments. Food is offered, but this is probably too broad a search criterion.

7. Cancel out of this screen and go back to the Keywords box.

8. Type **Drinks** into this box and click on Search.

You're offered a choice of seven different graphics. By using the Keywords option, we have narrowed our graphics search from 277 to 7. Pretty neat.

9. Click on the graphics offered and take a look. There are some great ones here. Celebrate 3, shown here, looks pretty good. So does Tropical Drinks. Let's go with that one.

You can pull down the names of more graphics libraries if you cannot find what you're looking for in this one. Print Shop Deluxe Ensemble II has some 4500 graphics available for your projects. We'll talk more about graphics and graphics libraries in Part III, "Managing Graphics."

10. With Tropical Drinks selected, click OK and you return to the main project window with Tropical Drinks inserted into the graphic placeholder.

11. Select the graphic and, holding down your left mouse button, drag it to the lower-left corner of the invitation, as shown here.

That completes the design for the front of our invitation. On it, we've told our friends three important things:

◆ The location of the party (i.e., the name of the ship it will be on)

◆ The kind of party we're having

◆ That refreshments will be served

We are now ready to start working on the inside spread page. We can get to the inside page by clicking on the right arrow on the lower-right corner of the screen, shown here. This is called the Navigation tool,

designed to move you from page to page of a multipage project. You'll only see it when you're working on greeting cards or postcards (the only multipage projects in Print Shop).

◆ Designing the Inside of the Card

Once you've selected the right arrow on the Navigation tool, Print Shop jumps right in and has you select a backdrop for the inside of the card.

Selecting a Backdrop

You'll see the Backdrops Browser again (the same dialog box you saw when you were designing the front of the card). Selecting a backdrop from those listed should be fairly easy since we've already established the look of the card with the design elements on the front. We just need to find an inside backdrop that matches or complements what we have already done.

The backdrop graphics listed are different from those offered for the front of the card. In this case, the inside of the card is twice the size of the front, and the graphics are sized to fit this new area.

Again, you're offered multiple libraries from which to choose your graphic. Also, you can again use the search options to find a graphic if you like. Let's take a look at those offered.

1. Click through the graphics so you can see them in preview. We

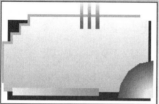

spotted one called Gradient, shown here. It has an art deco look to it that matches the background we put on the front.

2. Select Gradient and click OK.

Selecting a Layout

At this point the Select a Layout dialog box appears again. The layout options are different than when we designed the front of the card because the page size and expected content are different.

Deciding What Information to Include

Before we select a layout, let's decide what information we want to include so we can pick one that provides the right kind of placeholders. We've already provided the ship's name, but there are still some un-answered questions:

What date is the party?	Tuesday, November 4
When does the party start and when will it be over?	3 to 5 p.m.
Where is the ship located?	Pier 39 on the San Francisco Waterfront
Where on the ship will the party be held?	In our stateroom, number 112

We'll also want our friends to let us know if they plan to attend, so we'll need an RSVP line. And of course we want to let them know that they're invited, so we'll want a headline for that.

Basically, we need to have a layout with four placeholders for all the above information. We'll need a headline placeholder for the "you're invited" text, two text placeholders for the specifics (one for date and time, one for location), and one more headline placeholder for the RSVP.

Previewing the Layouts

With this information in mind, let's look at the layouts available. (If you can't find one you like, you can always make your own.) All of the choices offered, except one, give us the placeholders we need, so it's just a matter of which layout we like best.

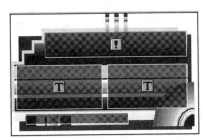

1. Choose Gradient 4, shown here.

2. Before confirming the layout, click on the box that says Lighten Backdrop. This will make the backdrop lighter and give more emphasis to the text.

When you do this, you are given 27 additional layout options. You can click through a few of these for practice, but stick with Gradient 4 as the selection.

3. When you're finished browsing, select Gradient 4 again and click OK. You return to the main project window with your layout in place.

Adding Text

Now let's fill the text and headline blocks. You can fill these just as you did on the front of the card. We've chosen to fill these blocks as shown

here, using a Double Arch Up headline.

1. Since you've now had some experience with text and headline blocks, try your hand at filling in the placeholders.

Feel free to experiment with different headline types, fonts, colors, whatever.

2. When you're finished with the inside of the card, click the right arrow of the Navigation tool to go to the back of the card.

◆ Designing the Back of the Card

Since this is the first time you've been to the back of the card, you are prompted to select a layout. (No backdrops are offered, since the back of a card is usually pretty sparse.)

1. Click through the layouts and you'll see that some offer text and graphics.

What we'd like to do is have one graphic, plus a text box where we can give directions to the party location. Layout 9 looks like it might work. We'll have to resize the text block to make it bigger, but that's easy enough.

2. Select Layout 9 and click OK.

Selecting a Graphic

Filling the blocks is easy to do. Let's do the graphic first.

1. Click on the bear icon and you go to the Graphics Browser dialog box. Note that you are working with a row graphic.

Since the *Wind Song* is a computerized sailing ship, let's look for a sailboat for the back of our card.

2. Change the Graphic Library area to All Libraries and type **Sailing** in the Keywords box.

3. Click on Search.

We're offered two graphics: Sailing Flags, shown here, and Seaside

Dining. Neither of these will work. Let's change the row graphic to a square graphic.

4. Click on the arrow next to Row Graphics and select Square Graphics, then All Libraries again.

Now you're presented with a choice of nine graphics. Click through them.

The first one named Sailboat would be okay. The second Sailboat, which is a cartoon sailboat, shown here, is not a choice we'd make. The one named Sailing looks just like what we had in mind. Let's select this one.

5. With Sailing selected, click OK; it is placed in the square placeholder on the back of the invitation.

Putting a Frame around the Text Box

We're going to fill the text block with directions, and a frame around the box might be nice. First, we'll need to make it bigger.

1. Click on it to select it, then pull on the handles to resize it.

2. Double-click on the *T* at its center, type the directions (you can just make up something for now), and click OK. You now have an unframed text box with the directions in it.

3. Select the text box once more and pull down the Object menu from the top of the screen.

4. Select Frame and choose a frame for the box. Let's choose Thick Line.

5. Click OK.

There, the box is framed and we are finished with this project. Check out Figure 1.9 to see what the invitation looks like.

Let's save the project:

1. Click on the File menu at the top of the screen, then select Save.

2. Name the file Windsong and click OK.

◆ Endnotes

Mission accomplished! You've completed your first Print Shop project, and a complicated one at that: a three-page greeting card. You have:

◆ Selected a project and chosen an orientation, a backdrop, and a layout for it

◆ Browsed for graphics

◆ Created and filled placeholders

◆ Worked in text and headline blocks

◆ Moved and resized objects

◆ Selected color for type

◆ Worked a bit with the main menu and with the toolbar

You've gotten your feet wet. In Chapter 2, "Discovering Tools," we'll get a bit more serious with a prolonged look at the toolbar. You've only just begun. The best is yet to come.

Front

Inside

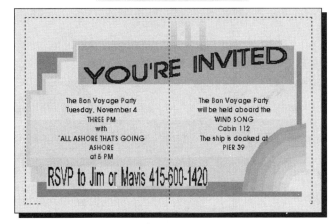

YOU'RE INVITED

The Bon Voyage Party
Tuesday, November 4
THREE PM
with
"ALL ASHORE THATS GOING
ASHORE
at 5 PM

The Bon Voyage Party
will be held aboard the
WIND SONG
Cabin 112
The ship is docked at
PIER 39

RSVP to Jim or Mavis 415-600-1420

Back

DIRECTIONS
TO THE PIER
1280 to 12th
Street. Go West to
15th and then
right to Pier 39.

Figure 1.9: Congratulations! You've completed your first Print Shop project.

CHAPTER TWO

Discovering Tools

Your mission: to discover everything there is to know about tools

◆

Print Shop is designed to be simple to use. With its graphic-oriented base, Print Shop lets you use the tools and menus to add individual creativity to a project. As you work your way through the book, you'll explore how to make maximum use of these tool and menu commands to customize your projects. We'll talk tools in this chapter and menus in the next.

◆ Starting the Project

In this chapter we'll explore each of the commands offered on the toolbar using a ready-made sign as our project.

1. If you have not opened Print Shop yet, open it now.

2. The first screen you see asks you to select a project. Click on Signs & Posters.

3. You are given two paths to choose from: Select a Ready Made or Start From Scratch. Click on Select a Ready Made.

4. Next, you're asked to select a sign theme: Home, Business, Celebration, Community, School, or All Themes (see Figure 2.1). Select Community.

You're presented with a list of ready-made signs. As you click on each file, you can see it in the preview area. For this project, we're looking for

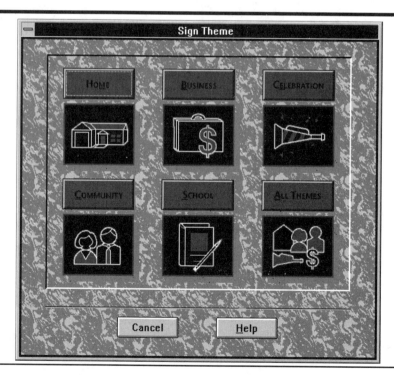

Figure 2.1:   Select a theme for your ready-made sign.

a sign that has graphics, text, headlines, a border, and graduated page coloring—or something along those lines. In other words, we're looking for a sign with lots of stuff on it, like the Car Wash sign (see Figure 2.2).

5. Click once on Car Wash and take a look at it in preview. Looks perfect. Click on Select.

Car Wash opens in the project window (see Figure 2.3), ready for you to try your hand with the tools.

 Ready-made projects are complete and can be printed out as is; however, you can personalize them by adding or deleting objects, changing the backdrop, altering the layout, changing the page color, or anything else.

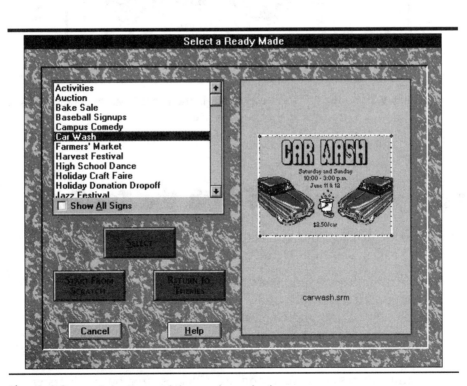

Figure 2.2:   Select one of the ready-made signs.

Figure 2.3:   The Car Wash sign opens in the project window, ready for you
to print as is or customize as you like.

◆ Getting Acquainted with the Toolbar

Now we're ready to begin. Let's take a look at the commands available on
the toolbar, shown in Figure 2.4.

On the toolbar are nine tools, an Item Selector, a Color Selector, and a
Shading Selector, which allow you to select, rotate, move, add, zoom,
delete, flip, frame, and color objects in your project.

Some of the toolbar options are also available in the menu bar at the
top of the window, but the layout of the toolbar makes often-used
commands easier to access and use. Clicking on a button is faster than
pulling down a menu command. Of the tools offered, New Object,
Zoom, Flip, and Frame have pop-up menus to help you define
exactly what you want to do.

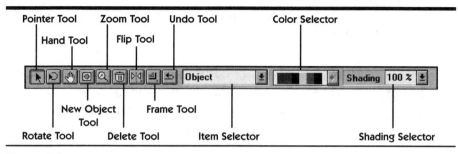

Figure 2.4:   The Print Shop toolbar

◆ Moving and Resizing Objects

Pointer Tool

The first tool—and the one you will use most often—is the Pointer tool. It allows you to select an object and then change that object in a variety of ways, including moving, resizing, coloring, shading, and inserting graphics or text.

Let's use the car wash sign to take a look at the many ways you can use the Pointer tool. You already have the project on-screen, so let's get to it.

Moving a Single Object

You can move an object easily using the Pointer tool. Let's try our hand at a few ways to move objects within a window.

1. Select the Pointer tool.

2. Click on the bucket. A box with black squares at each corner appears around the bucket, as shown here. These black squares are called *handles* because you can grab one of these and rotate or resize the object.

3. Again click on the bucket and, holding your left mouse button down, drag it to the upper-right corner of the sign. While you're moving the object, you'll see a box the size of the object making the move. The object and its handles will not move yet.

4. Once the box is in position, release the mouse button. The object jumps to its new location.

 All objects have four corners, regardless of what is inside the object area. The bucket, for example, appears to be just a bucket, but when you select it, you can see it is in a square box. The same would be true no matter what size and shape the graphics or text inside a box. The box always has four corners and four handles.

Moving Multiple Objects Together

Okay, we've moved a single object successfully. Now let's take a look at how we can move more than one object, keeping them in the same position in relationship to each other.

1. First, put the bucket back into its original position: just hold the left mouse button down and drag it back between the two cars.

Now let's move the bucket and the $2.50 text together.

2. Select the bucket with the Pointer tool.

3. Hold down the Shift key and click on the $2.50. Both objects are

 selected. You can tell because both have handles, as shown here.

4. Now hold down the left mouse button anywhere on either of the selected objects and drag both of them to the upper-right corner. Two box outlines appear and move together as you drag your mouse to the new location.

5. Release the mouse and both of the objects jump to their new location.

So now you know how to move multiple objects at once. Now drag both the bucket and the $2.50 back to their original position using the same technique and we will resize an object.

Resizing Graphics

You can resize an object, making it larger or smaller, maintaining the aspect ratio or changing it entirely. In other words, you can make a square bigger or you can reshape the square to make it a rectangle.

Changing a Graphic's Size

Let's do a little graphic resizing using the Pointer tool on the Car Wash sign.

1. Click on the Pointer tool and select the bucket.

2. Now place your mouse cursor on one of the handles and, holding the left mouse button down, pull out to make the object larger.

 When resizing an object, you select a handle to pull or push the object to its new size. The opposite handle becomes an anchor for the object and does not move from its original position as you resize. If, for example, you pull on the handle in the upper-right corner, all corners of the object except the lower-left one move.

 The object itself does not change as you pull on a handle. Rather, that same outlined box you saw when you moved an object does the resizing. When you release the mouse button, the object jumps to its new size, as shown here. Note that the aspect ratio of the bucket remains the same; it's just larger.

Aspect Ratio is the relationship between the width and the height of an object. For instance, the aspect ratio of the bucket in our sign appears to be 1:1, which means it is a square, just as wide as it is tall. We could resize it, making it larger but keeping it a square. Or we could reshape it, changing the aspect ratio by stretching it or squeezing it into another shape, say a rectangle.

3. We can make an object smaller in the same way. Do that now, pushing the bucket back to its original size.

Changing a Graphic's Shape

To resize an object, changing its aspect ratio:

1. Select the bucket.

2. Hold down the Ctrl key and the left mouse button at the same time, and push down on the upper-right handle. The bucket  changes its aspect ratio: the box becomes a rectangle and the bucket gets short and fat, as shown here.

3. Pull the bucket back to its original size, and we'll move on to headlines and text blocks.

Resizing Headline or Text Blocks

So that's how you resize a graphic, but what about headline or text blocks? Do you resize them the same way? The answer is yes and no.

To resize headline or text blocks, you do exactly the same thing you've done with the bucket, only the methods for resizing and reshaping are reversed. Let's try it.

Maintaining the Aspect Ratio

To resize a text or headline block without changing its aspect ratio:

1. Click on the Car Wash headline block to select it.

2. Hold down the left mouse button and the Ctrl key and pull the lower-left corner of the Car Wash headline down and to the left.

The square outline of the block appears as you pull it to a larger size, while still maintaining its aspect ratio.

Changing the Aspect Ratio

To resize a text or headline block, changing its aspect ratio:

1. Select the Car Wash headline block again.

2. Hold down the left mouse button and push the lower-left corner up.

The outline of the block appears as you change the size of the text block to a more elongated and smaller size. Text located inside a headline block will resize itself to fit in the block you make. Headline text is designed to fill the box.

On the other hand, text in a text block will *not* resize when you change the size of its box. Rather, the type will remain the same size and will only rearrange itself to fit in the box, if it can. If the type can no longer fit because the box is too small, it will disappear outside the box where you can no longer see it.

Let's see what happens when we make a text box smaller.

1. Click on the text box that begins with "Saturday and Sunday..."

2. Push on one of the handles, making the box smaller.

Some of the text disappears. It no longer fits in the box and is hidden

outside, as shown here. The text is not gone; it's just hidden. You can reclaim it by making the type smaller or the box larger.

Before we go on, drag all the objects in your Car Wash sign back into their original positions and shapes. Next we'll learn to rotate objects.

You can resize two or more objects simultaneously in exactly the same way that you would resize one by linking the items together. You link the objects together by selecting them all using the Pointer tool and your Shift key. If one of the objects in the linked objects is a graphic, you follow the procedure for resizing graphics. If all the objects in the linked objects are text or headline blocks, use the process for resizing text or headline blocks.

◆ Rotating Objects

Rotate Tool

The Rotate tool allows you to pivot objects on the handle you select. You can select and rotate one object or several objects at the same time.

Rotating a Single Object

Let's give it a try on the Car Wash sign.

1. Select the Rotate tool by clicking on it. Your cursor becomes a semi-circle with an arrow on one end (just like the Rotate tool button) when you move it into the window.

2. Now select the car on the left side by clicking on it with this arrow cursor. Handles appear at the four corners of the object.

3. To rotate the object, put the arrow directly on one of the handles and turn in a clockwise or counter-clockwise direction. The object rotates, as shown here.

4. Rotate the car back to its original position.

Rotating Multiple Objects Together

Like the Pointer tool, the Rotate tool allows you to select more than one object and turn them all at the same time. Try this.

1. Select the car at the left.

2. Hold down the Shift key and select the car at the right, then the bucket. You have now selected three objects.

3. Put the arrow cursor on any one of the handles on any one of the objects.

4. Now rotate. All three objects rotate together, maintaining their positioning from each other, as shown here.

5. Rotate until all objects are back in their original position.

◆ **Moving Around in the Document**

Hand Tool

Occasionally you'll want to view a project at a size larger than the main window allows. You can zoom in to focus on a certain part of the document, but then how do you see the parts that moved off-screen? The Hand tool allows you to move the document around in the window so you can see elements that may be hidden when the project is larger than the window.

 The Hand tool is not available when a project fits inside the viewing window, since no part of the project is hidden from view.

This is a handy option when you want to compose in actual size or larger than actual size to see colors or objects or text options better. Let's try using the Hand tool now. First we'll need to change how we are viewing the project.

1. Click on the Zoom tool (the magnifying glass), hold down the mouse button, and select Actual Size from the options offered.

The Car Wash sign no longer fits in the window, as shown in Figure 2.5. Note that the Hand tool changes from a shaded button to an outlined button to indicate that it is now available.

2. Click on the Hand tool. When you move your cursor back onto the document, you'll see a hand, indicating that this tool is active.

3. Now click anywhere on the sign and, holding down the left mouse button, move the hand cursor around. The document moves with the cursor so you can see the portions of it hidden outside the window.

Figure 2.5:   At actual size, the Car Wash sign no longer fits in the project window.

 You can also move around a project that is larger than the viewing window by using the scroll bars at the right and bottom edges of the window. Click on the button located inside the scroll bar and drag the button to move through the project. You'll notice that when you use the Hand tool, the scroll bars move as you move around.

Use the Zoom tool to change your view back so that the sign fits in the window, because we're off to add a few objects to the project using the New Object tool. See "Changing the View" later in the chapter for more about the Zoom tool.

◆ Adding Objects

New Object
Tool

With the New Object tool we can add objects to our project. A pop-up menu offers these choices: Graphic, Square Graphic, Row Graphic, Column Graphic, Text, Headline, Word Balloon, Horizontal Ruled Line, Vertical Ruled Line, Border, Mini-Border, Seal, Signature Block, Title Block, and Import....

When you select an option, a placeholder for the object will appear in the middle of your project page. Some options do not use a placeholder but rather place the object directly in the project.

Before we go on to actually adding the objects, let's find out what a placeholder is, what it does, what it looks like, and which objects are added using a placeholder.

Understanding Placeholders

Placeholders create a space for an object. Just as there are objects of different sizes and shapes, there are placeholders of different sizes and shapes. At the center of every placeholder is an icon that indicates what kind of placeholder it is. Placeholders and their default shapes and icons are as follows:

Square Graphic

Row Graphic
Column Graphic

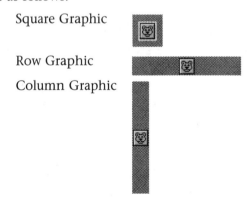

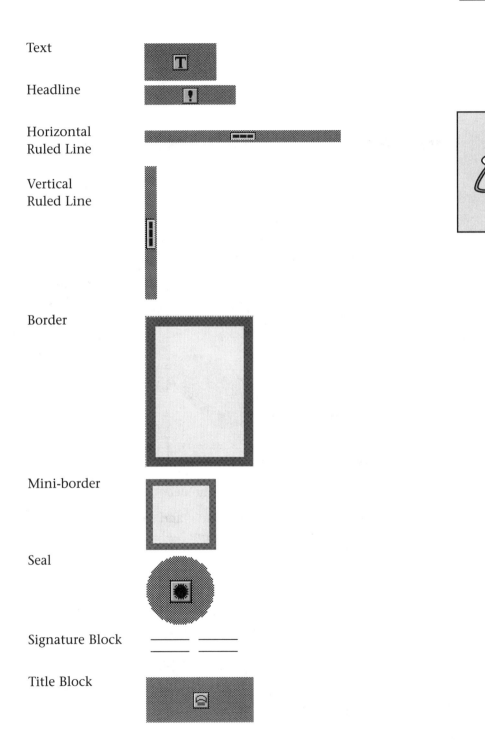

Text

Headline

Horizontal
Ruled Line

Vertical
Ruled Line

Border

Mini-border

Seal

Signature Block

Title Block

As we mentioned in Chapter 1, you fill a placeholder with an object by double-clicking on the placeholder, then either selecting a graphic or typing in text.

Adding Objects with Placeholders

Let's practice working with placeholders by adding a few objects to the Car Wash project.

1. Click on the New Object tool; a pop-up menu offers the choices listed in "Understanding Placeholders," plus Graphic (meaning all graphic shapes), Word Balloon, and Import (a graphic).

2. Select Square Graphic; a square placeholder appears, as shown here. The default position for a new object is the center of the project, so that's where the placeholder appears. You can always move it or resize it using the Pointer tool.

Let's select a graphic for the placeholder.

3. Double-click on the placeholder and the Graphics Browser appears. Scroll through the graphics and highlight Elephant Forgets, as shown in Figure 2.6.

4. Click OK.

You immediately return to the project window. The placeholder is gone and in its place is the Elephant Forgets graphic inside a box with handles. Now you can move and resize the new graphic as you did with the objects that were originally part of the sign.

We're going to learn a different way to add objects, so let's get the one we just added out of the way.

Figure 2.6: The Elephant Forgets graphic is shown in the preview window.

5. Select the Elephant Forgets graphic with the Pointer tool, then hit the Delete key on your keyboard. The graphic disappears.

Customizing Placeholders

Using the Ctrl key, you can add custom-sized placeholders for most of the objects offered by the New Object tool. That is, you can draw a placeholder to your own specifications before you insert the object in it. Custom-sized placeholders can be drawn for square graphics, row graphics, column graphics, text, headlines, horizontal ruled lines, vertical ruled lines, and mini-borders. You cannot customize a border or an imported graphic in this way.

Let's try it.

1. Hold down the Ctrl key and click on the New Object tool, then select the object type. Again, let's add a square graphic.

2. Release the Ctrl key and the mouse button and move your cursor into the project area. A small box appears as your cursor.

3. Click in the upper-right corner of the sign, then drag down and to the left. A box appears and follows your movement as you drag. When the box fills the space to the right of the large Car Wash headline, release the mouse button.

You can continue to create custom-sized placeholders for square graphics until you select another tool or a different object. Practice drawing placeholders until you've got the hang of it. When you're done, delete any extra placeholder boxes you've added. Leave only the one we drew first in the upper-right corner of the sign.

4. Double-click on the bear icon in the remaining placeholder and insert the Elephant Forgets graphic, as shown here.

◆ Changing the View

Zoom Tool

As we've already discovered, we can change our view of the project using the Zoom tool. When you click on the Zoom tool, a pop-up menu offers you the options of Zoom In, Zoom Out, Fit to Window, 25%, 50%, Actual Size, 150%, and 200%. You will find it a convenience to be able to change the view in order to work on more detailed aspects of the project.

Let's take a closer look at the elephant.

1. Click on the Zoom tool and select 200%. The project becomes bigger than the window so we can no longer see all of it.

2. Click on the Hand tool and move the project window around until you can see the elephant.

3. Select the elephant and adjust it as necessary (resize it, move it around, whatever you need to do) to better fit it on the page next to the Car Wash headline, as shown in Figure 2.7.

4. Click on the Zoom tool again and change the view back to Fit to Window.

Figure 2.7:   Zoom in to 200% so you can better see the elephant's position on the page.

◆ Deleting Objects

Delete Tool

The icon for the Delete tool is, appropriately, a trash can. Anything highlighted is deleted when you click on this button.

Give deleting a try.

1. Select the elephant, then click on the Delete tool. The elephant disappears.

2. Now click on the Undo tool and the elephant returns to its former position.

If you wish to undelete the last deletion, click on the Undo tool, the U-shaped arrow on the toolbar. Only the last thing you deleted can be restored. See "Undoing or Redoing Your Last Action" later in the chapter for more on the Undo tool.

◆ Flipping Objects

Flip Tool

The Flip tool does just what you'd expect: it lets you flip an object horizontally, vertically, or both. This gives you a lot of flexibility with graphics.

Let's give it a try.

1. Using the Pointer tool, select the car on the left side.

2. Click on the Flip tool. A pop-up menu appears, offering you the choice of Horizontal, Vertical, or Both. Note that when you begin, the car is facing toward the right.

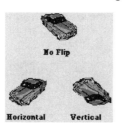

No Flip

Horizontal   Vertical

3. Click Horizontal, and the car faces left. Then click Vertical, and the car turns upside-down, as shown here.

4. To return the car to its original position, select Both from the Flip menu. It flips both vertically and horizontally and once again faces right.

◆ Framing Objects

Frame Tool

As the name indicates, the Frame tool allows you to put frames around objects. You can frame any object except a border, mini-border, seal, or ruled line. When you click on this icon, a pop-up menu offers None, Thin Line, Thick Line, Double Line, or Drop Shadow. If the object already has a frame, a check mark appears next to one of these selections.

Let's add a frame to the bucket.

1. Select the bucket.

2. Click on the Frame tool. You'll note that on the pop-up menu, None is checked, indicating that the object does not have a frame.

3. Click on Thin Line. The menu goes away and the frame appears around the graphic.

Experiment with the different frames offered by the Frame tool. All the framing options are shown in Figure 2.8.

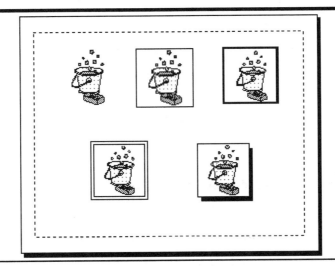

Figure 2.8:   Your framing choices are No Frame, Thin Line, Thick Line, Double Line, and Drop Shadow.

4. When you're done, select None from the Frame menu to return the bucket to its original state.

Note that the frames you've just added are black. This is the default color for frames. You can change this color, choosing from a selection of different colors offered on the palette in the Color Selector. We'll talk about that in "Coloring and Shading an Area" later in this chapter.

◆ Undoing or Redoing Your Last Action

Undo Tool

The Undo tool reverses the last action you performed. It can act as both an Undo tool to reverse the last action and a Redo tool to reverse the last Undo command.

Undoing Your Last Action

Use the Undo tool to reverse your last action, whether it was deleting, moving, changing a color, changing a backdrop, or anything else.

Let's try the Undo tool on a graphic change.

1. Double-click on the bucket, and the Graphics Browser opens.

2. Select a new graphic (any one will do) and click OK. The new graphic you selected replaces the bucket.

3. Click on the Undo tool, and the graphic changes back to the bucket.

Redoing Your Last Action

If you change your mind again, never fear. The Undo tool becomes a Redo tool immediately after an Undo command. Let's give it a try.

1. Click on the Undo tool. The graphic you selected to replace the bucket reappears, since this was your last undo in the exercise above.

2. Click on the Undo tool again and the bucket returns.

If you've performed any actions after clicking the Undo tool, the tool will not act as a Redo tool; instead, clicking it will undo the most recent change.

◆ Coloring and Shading an Area

With the next three items on the toolbar—the Item Selector, the Color Selector, and the Shading Selector, shown below—you can change the color of an object or the shading of a multicolored object.

First you must select what you want to shade or color. Then, using the Item Selector, choose which area of that object you want to apply the shading or color to. The choices offered by the Item Selector will vary depending on the object selected:

Object	Options
Graphic	Object
	Behind Object
	Frame
	Page
	Page Blend
Signature Block	Signature Text
	Autograph
	Behind Object
	Page
	Page Blend
Text	Text
	Behind Text
	Frame
	Page
	Page Blend
Word Balloon	Text
	Balloon
	Page
	Page Blend

No Object	Page
	Page Blend
	Backdrop (if one is part of the project)

Make your choice, then change the color with the Color Selector or the shading with the Shading Selector.

 You cannot change colors for a multicolored object, but you can change the saturation of these colors in increments of 10%. The lower the percentage, the lighter the color.

Now let's change our sign using the Item Selector, the Color Selector, and the Shading Selector.

1. Select one of the cars with the Pointer tool.

2. Select Object from the Item Selector.

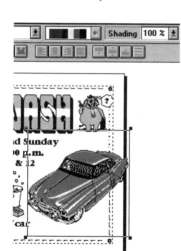 The Color Selector changes to multiple colors, as shown here (in grayscale, it appears as various shades of gray), because the car is more than one color. Note also that the Shading Selector reads 100%. We cannot change the color of the car because it is multicolored, but we can change the color saturation.

3. Click on the arrow at the right edge of the Shading Selector. A menu pops up, offering options from 10% to 100%. Click on 50% and see the car change to a lighter shade.

4. To change the color of the area behind the object, select Behind Object from the Item Selector. The color in the Color Selector reads Clear. This is the present color of the area behind the object. The Shading Selector has become light in color, meaning that it is not available for use, while the Color Selector is dark in color, indicating that it is available.

5. Click on the arrow in the right corner of the Color Selector and a color palette pops up, offering a wide choice of colors. Run your cursor over the color palette; the color in the Color Selector changes as you move around the color palette. Select one of the colors, say green. The color of the area behind the car changes to your choice.

6. To add a colored frame to the car, select the Frame tool from the toolbar and put a thick line frame around the car. Select Frame from the Item Selector and you'll see that the color of the frame is black. Change it by clicking on the Color Selector and selecting a new color, say blue.

You have just put your multicolored car into a green box with a thick blue line around it. Cool.

 In some cases, the graphic may cover the entire object area. When this happens, you cannot color behind the object because there is no area behind the object that you can see.

The Page option on the Item Selector always refers to the full page of the project. You can color this and shade the color, provided the backdrop does not cover the entire page. Our Car Wash sign does not have a backdrop and the page is colored. Click on any part of the page and take a look at the Color Selector. You'll see that the page is a shade of yellow. We can change the color of the page with the Color Selector just as we changed the area behind the car.

The Page Blend option blends two different colors in a pattern across the page. The Item Selector is used only to select the two colors; the actual blend is done using the Project menu. We'll take a more in-depth look at page blending in Chapter 3.

Selected text can be colored using the Item Selector and the Color Selector, but headlines cannot. Headlines can only be colored in the Headline dialog box.

◆ Endnotes

Mission accomplished. You now know everything there is to know about the Print Shop toolbar. You can:

- ◆ Select, rotate, move, add, flip, frame, or color an object
- ◆ Zoom in or out of a project
- ◆ Add color to a page, object, or background
- ◆ Delete and undo

You're a toolbar expert. Now on to the main menu to see how it works with the toolbar. Do not close your Car Wash sign. We'll be using it in Chapter 3, "Mastering Menus."

Mastering Menus

Your mission: to learn the main menu backward and forward

◆

Print Shop's main menu, shown below, offers all the commands that the toolbar does, plus more. It trades the one-click convenience of the tool-bar for a more complete list of command options.

File	Edit	Object	Project	View	Extras	Help

You can open, print, save, view, or change a project in numerous ways from the main menu.

In order to look at the main menu, you need to open a file. The Car Wash sign from Chapter 2 should still be open. If it's not, open it again following the instructions in Chapter 2. The main menu bar appears above the toolbar across the top of the project window.

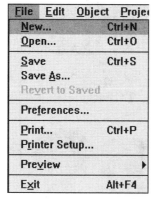

To access a menu command, click on an item, such as File, in the main menu. A submenu listing various commands drops down, as shown here; click on any of these commands to select it. A command followed by an ellipsis (...), like New, brings up a dialog box when you select it, while a command followed by a triangular-shaped arrow ('), like Preview, brings up a secondary drop-down menu. If a command is light gray in color, like Revert to Saved, it is currently unavailable.

 Some commands can also be accessed using keyboard shortcuts. Where applicable, these shortcuts are noted next to the corresponding menu commands. For example, in the File menu you can see that the keyboard shortcut for the Open command is Ctrl+O. The next time you want to open a project, you can just press Ctrl+O instead of selecting File ➤ Open.

◆ Using the File Menu

File menu commands perform housekeeping chores such as starting a new document, opening an already existing document, selecting project preferences, saving and printing a project, and exiting the program. These commands are generally the same as those in other programs (such as word processing programs), with some slight differences specific to Print Shop.

Let's take a look at the File menu's 10 commands: New, Open, Save, Save As, Revert To Saved, Preferences, Print, Printer Setup, Preview, and Exit.

Starting a New Project

Print Shop can only open one project at a time. Thus, if you are working on a project when you click on New, Print Shop closes the open project

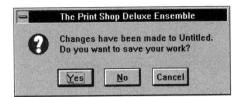

to make room for the new one. If you haven't saved the open document, a dialog box like the one shown here pops up. If you have not made any changes to the active project since you last saved it, this dialog box does not appear and the project closes automatically.

1. With the Car Wash sign open, select File ➤ New.

2. Click No at the Do you want to save? prompt.

The Select a Project dialog box appears. We just lost any changes we made to the Car Wash sign, but it still exists as a ready-made sign. So let's just open it again.

3. Click on Signs & Posters and reopen the ready-made Car Wash sign.

Opening an Existing File

The Open command in the File menu opens an existing Print Shop file. As with the New command, if you have an open project, a dialog box asks if you want to save your changes or just exit without saving.

1. With the Car Wash sign open, select File ➤ Open. If you have made changes to the Car Wash sign, a dialog box will ask if you want to save your changes. If you have made no changes, no prompt will appear.

The File Open dialog box appears. All project types are listed in the lower-left corner of the dialog box.

2. Select Greeting Cards from the Project Type box and all the greeting card projects appear in the Files box above. The Wind Song invitation from Chapter 1 is listed as one of the files available.

3. Click once on windsong.pdg. As you can see in Figure 3.1, the front page of the invitation is displayed in the preview area.

In addition to your own projects, you can preview and open all the ready-made projects provided by Print Shop.

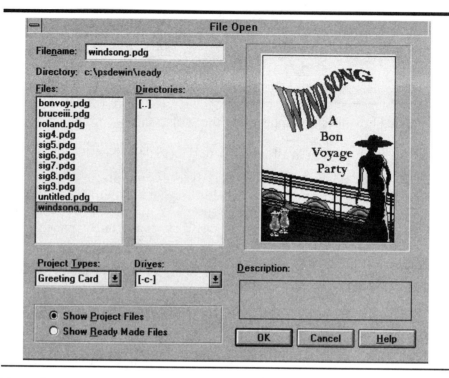

Figure 3.1: When you click on the windsong file, you can preview the first page before you open it.

4. Click on Show Ready Made Files at the bottom of the dialog box, then select the project type; all the ready-made files for that project appear in the Files area.

5. Click on a file to see it in the Preview area.

6. Select Cancel from the File Open dialog box and you revert to the Car Wash sign.

Saving a File

This command saves an active file for the first time or updates a file already saved.

1. Click on File ➤ Save.

If the project has been saved before and already has a file title, no prompt appears. The active file is simply updated. If the project has not been saved previously (and therefore does not have a file name), the File Save As dialog box appears.

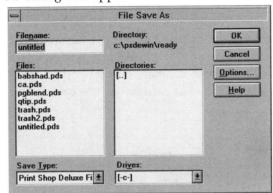

2. To save the file, type **CAR** in the Filename box, replacing *untitled*. The file type will be selected for you based on the project type. CAR is a sign so it will be saved with the extension .pds.

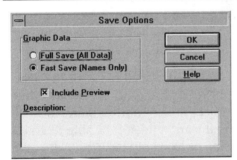

3. Click on the Options button to access the Save Options dialog box, shown here.

The Graphic Data section of this dialog box allows you to choose between Full Save (All Data), which is the default, or Fast Save (Names Only), which speeds up each save and takes up less disk space. The Include Preview check box lets you choose whether to show a preview of the project when you click on it in the File Open dialog box. Again, you might wish to uncheck Include Preview in order to speed up saves. Finally, you can include a description of the project in the Description box below if you choose.

4. Click on OK and you return to the File Save As dialog box.

The default file format in the Save Type box in the lower-left corner is Print Shop Deluxe File. You can also save the file as a Windows Metafile, a TIFF Bitmap File, or a Windows Bitmap File.

Note the directory where the file is being saved. The default is c:\psdewin (Print Shop Deluxe for Windows); since it's a ready-made project it will be saved in \ready. A project you created from scratch would be saved in c:\psdewin\projects. If you want the project saved to a different drive or directory, just type in where you want it to go or use your mouse to point and click your way through the drive and directory choices.

5. Once you've made your selections, click on OK to save the file.

Once the file is saved, the File Save As dialog box will disappear and the newly saved file will remain active. Whenever you click Save after this, the file will be saved automatically using the options you selected above; you won't see the File Save As dialog box again. If you want to change the save options, you need to use the Save As command, as explained in the next section.

Saving As

To change the save options of an already saved file, click on Save As. This brings up the File Save As dialog box, and you can select your preferences as before. For projects not previously saved, you can use either Save or Save As to give the file a name and location.

You can also rename or reroute an already saved file with the Save As command. This is a good way to experiment without endangering the original file. You can save the project under another name or in another location, make all the changes you want, and still be able to access the original project under its old name or in its old location. Let's save the CAR file under a new name.

1. Click on Save As. As with a first-time save, the File Save As dialog box appears.

2. Type **CAR2** in the Filename box.

3. Select any preferences you have from the Save Options dialog box and click on OK to return to the File Save As box.

4. Click on OK to save the file under its new name.

Now you can experiment on CAR2 as you please without ruining CAR. This procedure isn't really necessary with the ready-made CAR, but if you've spent hours perfecting your own project you can recognize the value of saving under another name.

Reverting to a Previously Saved Version

Another way to protect your original project is using the Revert to Saved command. When you choose this option, any changes you made in a document since the last time you saved it are ignored and the document reverts to what it was the last time you saved it. When you click on Revert to Saved, a dialog box gives you the opportunity to change your mind.

Choosing Preferences

Clicking on the Preferences option in the File menu brings up the

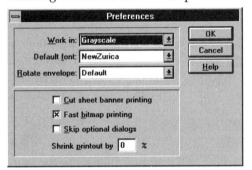

Preferences dialog box, shown here, which lets you change certain defaults in the Print Shop program.

Before we select the preferences, let's open a new file. Select File ➤ New, choose Banner, and select the ready-made file called School Open House. Note that you have opened a three-page banner. Dotted lines separate the pages, as shown here.

Okay, we have our working project. Let's take a look at the preferences.

1. Select File ➤ Preferences.

2. In the Preferences dialog box, select Grayscale from the Work in box. (If you are printing in black and white, you might want to work in grayscale instead of color so you have a better idea of how your project is actually going to look.)

3. Click on OK. The dialog box disappears and the banner changes from color to grayscale.

4. Select File ➤ Preferences again to reopen the Preferences dialog box. We'll cover the rest of the preferences without actually changing them.

The next option is the default font. The designated default font is used for headlines and text blocks that do not have a font set by the layout or by you. Change this if you like.

After that is an option called Rotate envelope. This option is used only if you are having problems printing envelopes. At the Default setting the program will adjust the rotation of the envelope output according to the printer you are using. At the Always setting, the program will always rotate the output 180 degrees. At the Never setting, the output will never be rotated.

If you are printing a banner, you can tell Print Shop to print on a cut sheet printer (such as a laser printer) rather than a continuous feed printer. If you're having difficulty printing on a continuous feed printer, select this option to tell Print Shop to treat your printer as a cut sheet printer.

The next option, Fast bitmap printing, is selected by default. This preference may solve printing problems if you have a dot matrix printer and you are having difficulty flipping or rotating bitmap graphics.

Select Skip optional dialogs for a more direct route to the main project window. If you select this option, you will bypass the Select a Path, Backdrops Browser, and Select a Layout dialog boxes (except if you're working with banners, labels, or calendars). With this option, you'll need only to select a project and then choose an orientation. You might want to do this if you're importing backdrops or other objects or if you want to create your own layout.

Finally, you can shrink the size at which Print Shop prints if you are having difficulty printing the entire image. If the image is being cut off on the edges, shrink the image slightly to solve the problem. Note that the option is phrased "Shrink printout *by*," not "Shrink printout *to*," so, for example, be sure to type 5% if you want the image to print at 95% of its original size.

5. Select Color again in the Work in box and click OK to return things to normal.

Printing a Project

When you click on Print, the Print dialog box, shown here, appears. Here

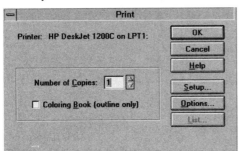

you can choose how many copies will print by clicking on the arrows or typing a number between 1 and 999 in the Number of Copies text box. In some projects you can also type a number from 10 to 400 in the Scale Percentage text box to have the document print at anywhere from

10 to 400 percent of its actual size. A project printed at 400 percent will print on 4 pages; a project at 300 percent, on 3 pages; and a project at 200 percent, on 2 pages. This option is not available for banners, so it does not appear on the Print dialog box shown here.

So far the print options have been pretty conventional. One of the interesting exceptions is the ability to print a project as a coloring book image, that is, in outline only. Let's give it a whirl.

1. Select File ➤ Print. The Print dialog box appears.

2. Click on the Coloring Book (outline only) check box and click OK. The image prints without a preview.

The Print dialog box also includes buttons labeled Setup, Options, and List. Setup is used to choose the settings for your particular printer, which is beyond the scope of this book. List lets you open a name, address, or custom list to merge to a project (see Chapter 11, "Creating and Merging Lists," for more information). Let's take a closer look at Options.

1. Click on Options to access the Print Options dialog box, shown here.

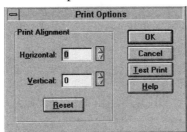

Here you can adjust the print alignment to better align the project on the page, moving the project in small increments up to one inch with the inch divided into 15 parts. You can set the alignment between –15 to +15, nudging the project up or down or right or left. (The effects vary from printer to printer.) The Reset button resets alignment to zero.

2. To test the alignment of your project on the page, click on Test Print, then OK. The dialog box closes and "Welcome to Print Shop Deluxe Ensemble II" prints with a box outline around the outer edges of the print page. In the case of the three-page banner, Test Print will print on three pages with a box outline around the outer edge of each page.

The Print dialog box offers additional options for certain projects. See Chapter 5, "Understanding Print Shop Projects," and Chapter 12, "Printing Made Easy," for information about printing specific projects.

Setting Up Your Printer

When you click on Printer Setup, a dialog box allows you to set up your printer. The options offered are specific to your printer. Since we may not have the same printer as you, we'll pass on discussing this here. If you need help, consult your Windows manual or ask somebody who knows about printer settings.

Previewing a Project

To preview a project in full screen before you print it out, select from the choices offered on the Preview pop-up list, shown here. You can preview a project in color, in black and white, or in coloring book format. Let's

take a look at the Open House banner in coloring book format.

1. Select File ➤ Preview.

2. From the Preview pop-up list, click on Coloring Book. Open House is previewed in coloring book format, as shown below. When you're finished looking, click on Done.

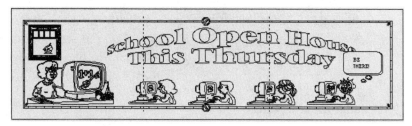

3. Click File ➤ Preview again and select Black and White to preview the banner in black and white. Click on Done.

4. Click File ➤ Preview and select Color to preview in color.

5. Click on Done to return to the main project window for the next File menu command, Exit.

Exiting the Program

Exit, the last command on the File menu, exits the Print Shop program. (Don't do this now! We're not done exploring the menus.) If you have not saved your project (or if you have not saved your most recent changes to a project), a prompt will ask you if you want to save it. If you click on Yes, you'll be asked to name the file (unless you have previously saved and named it). If you have saved your project and all its edits, or if you're working with a ready-made project and you haven't changed anything, Print Shop will close without a prompt.

◆ Using the Edit Menu

The Edit menu offers the following options: Undo, Cut, Copy, Paste, Delete, Duplicate, and Select All. These commands are pretty self-explanatory, but let's run through them quickly.

You must select an object before you can use most of the Edit commands. If no object is selected, the only edit option available is Select All.

Undoing an Action

Undo reverses your last action. If you delete something or make a change in the project and then change your mind, just select Edit ➤ Undo. You can undo an insertion, a deletion, a move, a color change, or anything else you've done. Keep in mind, though, that Undo only works for your most recent action. You cannot use it to put things back the way they were three actions ago.

The Undo command changes to match the last action. For example, if you delete an object, the Undo command reads Undo Delete Object. If you change the backdrop, the Undo command reads Undo Backdrop Change. If you change a color, the command reads Undo Color Change, and so on.

1. Click on the Pointer tool, then select the large graphic in the Open House banner that includes the teacher and the students.

2. From the Edit menu, click on Delete; the graphic is deleted.

3. Now from the Edit menu, select Undo Delete Object and the graphic returns.

Once you have used Undo, the command changes to Redo. For example, if you delete an object and then click on Undo Delete Object, the command will change to read Redo Delete Object. If you click on it, the object will be deleted again.

4. Pull down the Edit menu again; the Undo command now says Redo. Click on Redo Delete Object and the teacher and students disappear again.

5. Undo the deletion again to put the banner back the way it was.

Cutting Objects

The Cut command removes whatever is highlighted and stores it in the Clipboard (a Windows temporary storage area), where it remains until it is replaced. Once you have placed material in the Clipboard, you can paste it elsewhere in the document (or in another document) with the Paste command. The Cut command competes for storage in the Clipboard with the Copy command; every time you use the Cut or Copy command, the Clipboard erases what it has stored previously and replaces it with the new material.

When using the Cut command, make sure you paste the material in its new location as quickly as possible to prevent losing it in case you forget and cut or copy some new material. The Cut command is a good way to move material from one project to another or move material to a program other than Print Shop, assuming the file formats are compatible.

Using the Open House banner, we'll practice cutting.

1. Click on the object on the very front of the teacher's desk. (If you change your view to Actual Size, you'll see that this is a graphic of a lunch, an apple, and some books.

2. Click on Edit ➤ Cut and the object disappears. The lunch graphic is now stored in the Clipboard.

3. Since we're not quite ready to paste it, select Edit ➤ Undo to put the graphic back where it was.

Copying Objects

The Copy command makes a copy of whatever is highlighted and stores it in the Clipboard to be pasted elsewhere. Unlike a cut item, an item that is copied remains in the project. Every time you use the Copy command, the last item copied to the Clipboard is replaced by the new item. As noted already, Cut and Copy compete for the storage space in the Clipboard, so if you copy right after you cut, the item copied will replace the item cut.

Again using the Open House banner, let's copy the lunch graphic. You should still be in Actual Size view.

1. Click on the lunch graphic.

2. Click on Edit ➤ Copy and the object is copied. The original does not change at all.

The lunch graphic is now stored in the Clipboard. We'll paste it in the next section.

Pasting Objects

The Paste command pastes whatever is stored in the Clipboard into a project wherever you place the cursor. If nothing is stored in the Clipboard, the Paste command is light gray in color, indicating that it is unavailable.

We just copied the lunch graphic, so let's paste it now.

1. Click on Paste. The second lunch graphic is placed on top of the first one. The lunch graphic on top is selected, waiting for you to move it to its new location.

2. Drag the lunch graphic to the desk of the last child, as shown here.  (Just drag the graphic off the right edge of the screen; the window will scroll to the images on the right side of the project as you drag.) Now both the teacher and the last child have a lunch.

Deleting Objects

The Delete command serves the same function as the trash can icon on the toolbar and the Delete key on the keyboard. It erases whatever is highlighted or selected by the Pointer tool.

Let's delete the teacher's lunch.

1. Change the view back to Fit to Window so you can see the whole project at once.

2. Click on the teacher's lunch.

3. Click on Edit ➤ Delete. Now the teacher has no lunch.

Don't worry about the teacher. We'll return her lunch (or at least one just like it) when we duplicate objects in the next section.

Duplicating Objects

The Duplicate command makes one copy of the item(s) selected, placing it on top of and to the side of the item duplicated. Multiple copies can be made by continuing to click on Duplicate once you've selected an object. Use the Pointer tool to move the duplicated object into its desired location in the project.

Let's use Duplicate to give the teacher back her lunch.

1. Click on the child's lunch.

2. Select Edit ➤ Duplicate. A second lunch is created and placed on top of the first.

3. The lunch on top is selected by default. Drag it to the teacher's desk.

Selecting All

The Select All command selects everything in the project, including text, headlines, and graphics. Once selected, you can copy, cut, or duplicate everything with one command.

 You can use the Select All command to identify all the objects in a project. This is particularly useful when you're working with a ready-made project and are not quite sure, for example, where one text block ends and another begins or whether an image is one large graphic or a combination of several graphics.

Let's select everything in the Open House banner.

1. Click on Select All and all objects acquire boxes and handles, as shown below.

2. Click on any object and drag everything off the banner area.

You'll notice that two objects are left on the banner, as shown below.

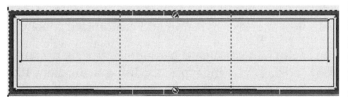 One is a box that is permanently locked. (You can tell it's locked because its handles are smaller

and lighter in color.) This box is the banner layout, and while you can add objects to the layout, you cannot delete portions of it. The other unmovable object is the border. Borders cannot be moved or changed in any way.

3. Pull down the Edit menu and select Undo Move Object; your banner returns to its previous state.

◆ Using the Object Menu

The Object menu lets you add or manipulate objects in your project. The Object menu commands are Add, Edit, Shadow, Border Size, Frame, Order, Scale, Rotate, Flip, Lock, Unlock, and Align. Many of the commands offered in this menu are also available in the toolbar, including the commands under Add, Frame, Rotate (with some variations), and Flip. The others are available only from this menu.

Adding Objects

The Add command offers the following choices: Graphic, Square Graphic, Row Graphic, Column Graphic, Text, Headline, Word Balloon, Horizontal Ruled Line, Vertical Ruled Line, Border, Mini-border, Seal, Signature Block, Title Block, and Import (a graphic). Do these commands look familiar? They should: they are exactly the same—and function the same way—as the options for the New Object tool on the toolbar. Please refer to "Adding Objects" in Chapter 2 for details.

Editing Objects

You can edit an object by selecting it and clicking on Object ➤ Edit. If the object selected is a graphic, you will see a dialog box that allows you to select a new graphic, replacing the current one. If the object selected is a text or headline block, you'll see a dialog box that allows you to change the font, color, and text style and add customized touches.

You can also trigger the Edit command by double-clicking on any object. Let's take a look at different types of editing using the Object ➤ Edit menu.

Replacing a Graphic

First, let's edit a graphic.

1. In the banner, select the small graphic inside the window graphic above the teacher's head. It's hard to see exactly what this is, but since handles appear around it when you click on it, you know it is a separate graphic, not part of the window graphic. If you have problems selecting this small graphic, move the window graphic aside so you can grab the small one without interference.

2. Select the View menu and change the view to 150%. Now you can see that the small graphic is a house.

3. Select Edit from the Object menu or double-click on the graphic. The Graphics Browser dialog box pops up.

4. Select the Cat in Window graphic to replace the house.

5. Click OK and you return to the project window. The Cat in Window graphic has replaced the house.

6. Resize the graphic to fill the window, as shown here, by pulling on its handles. Move it around until it fits in the window.

Editing Text

Now let's edit some text. First, pull down the View menu and select Fit to Window so you can see the complete banner.

1. Now select the text block that says, "BE THERE!" (This is the only text block in this banner. The other text is in a headline block.)

2. Click on Object ➤ Edit and the Edit Text dialog box appears. This is the same dialog box that appeared in Chapter 1 when we added text to the front of the party invitation.

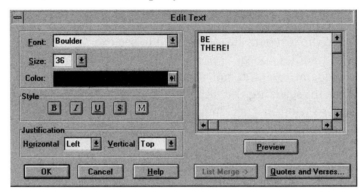

The selected text from the project is in the box to the right and all its specifications are noted: font, size, color, style, and justification. You can change any of these specifications and you can add or delete text. Clicking on the Preview button will accurately preview the text's font, size, color, and style in the text box.

Let's change the text:

3. Delete BE THERE! in the text box and type **I taut I taw a puddy cat!**

4. Click on Preview and the new text is previewed.

5. Click OK and you return to your project with the new text in place. You'll note the text does not fit in the word bubble graphic anymore. To make the bubble bigger, select it, then pull on its handles until it's big enough for the text to fit inside. If you have trouble working with the bubble and the text at this size, zoom in for a better view.

Editing Headlines

Now let's edit the headline block.

1. Select the School Open House headline block.

2. Click on Object ➤ Edit and the Headline dialog box appears, as shown below. This is the same dialog box that appeared in Chapter 1

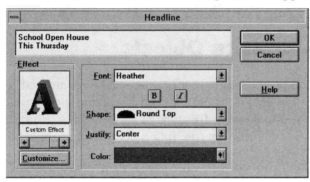

when we added the headline to the front of the party invitation. The banner headline appears in the top preview box and all its specifications, including effect, font, shape, justification, and color, are noted below.

3. Click on the arrow to the right of the Shape box and a list drops down offering 21 different headline shapes. Change the headline shape from Round Top to Fan.

4. Now click on Customize and the Custom Effect dialog box appears

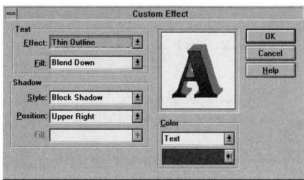

(we saw this dialog box in Chapter 1, too). Here you have even more options for changing the type's effect, fill, shadow, position, color, color saturation, and more. (For more information, see Chapter 10, "Working with Text and Headlines.")

5. Change the Fill box from Blend Down to Radiant and click OK; you return to the Headline dialog box.

6. Click OK again and you return to the banner with a new headline shape and fill, as shown below.

Adding Shadows to Objects

The next option on the Object menu is the Shadow command. You can add shadows to square, row, and column graphics, giving the graphics a somewhat three-dimensional look. This type of shadow differs from the shadow you can put behind a frame in that it falls behind the graphic itself.

Let's take a look at shadows. First, let's add a square graphic to the Open House banner.

1. From the Object menu, select Add, then click on Square Graphic. A placeholder for a square graphic is added to the banner.

2. Double-click on the bear icon in the center of the square graphic. The Graphics Browser pops up.

3. Click on Baby and then OK. The Baby graphic is placed in the square graphic box.

4. Drag the baby so it's dancing on top of the teacher's computer screen, as shown here.

5. Now pull down the Object menu and select Shadow, then On. The baby now has a shadow.

Not all graphics benefit from the Shadow option. Some have so many elements in them that adding a shadow just confuses the subject. Others have built-in shadows, making an additional shadow unnecessary. The size of the graphic on the project page will be a factor in whether the shadow works or not. Obviously, on larger graphics a shadow will be more visible than on smaller ones.

It's best to take a look at graphics with and without shadows to see if the effect works. The baby is shown here with and without a shadow. Does

the shadow add anything to the graphic? (You may wish to change the view to a larger size in order to see better.) If you decide it does not, you can reverse the procedure by selecting either Object ä Shadow ➤ Off or Edit ➤ Undo.

NO SHADOW   SHADOW

Framing an Object

The Frame command in the Object menu has the same options and works the same way as the Frame tool on the toolbar. For specifics, please refer to "Framing Objects" in Chapter 2.

Putting Objects in Order

Print Shop's default is for the last object placed on the page to be the uppermost object, covering the objects below it. But if, for example, you want text to print on top of a graphic or one graphic to print over a portion of another graphic, you can use the Order command to designate the objects' order of placement.

The Order commands available and their designated functions are as follows:

Bring Forward	Moves object forward one layer
Bring to Front	Moves object to the topmost layer
Send Backward	Moves object backward one layer
Send to Back	Moves object to bottommost layer

You cannot place objects behind the backdrop; it will always be the bottom layer of the project. And you cannot place objects in front of a border; it will always be the top layer. (If you really want to place objects in front of a border, there's a way around this: make a mini-border and stretch it to fit the page. You *can* place objects in front of a mini-border.)

1. Click on the baby graphic.

2. Select Behind Object from the Item Selector in the toolbar and change the color behind the baby from Clear to a color you like. Since the background is now colored, you can't see through it and the baby appears in a square.

3. Drag the baby down over the large classroom graphic to cover the teacher's computer screen. Resize the graphic box to fit the screen, as shown here. The baby graphic is now in front of the larger classroom graphic.

4. Select Order from the Object menu and click on Send to Back. The baby disappears. Click on the classroom graphic and drag it to the top of the banner. You'll see that the baby is behind it, as shown below.

5. Select the baby again. From the Object menu, click on Order ➤ Bring to Front.

6. Now move the larger classroom graphic back into position and the baby is back in its position on-screen.

Scaling an Object

So far we've resized objects by selecting them and pulling or pushing on their handles. Another way is to use the Scale command, which scales objects by a specific percentage. This is a good way to fit an object precisely into a given space, such as the baby in the computer screen.

1. Select the child's lunch graphic.

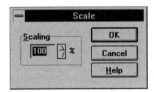

2. Select Object ➤ Scale. The Scale dialog box, shown here, appears.

The percentage defaults to 100%, representing the object's current size. You can either type the percentage you want or use the arrow keys to move the percentage up or down. When you scale a graphic or headline box, the graphic or headline changes its size to fit into the new box. When you scale a text box, only the box changes its size. The text remains the same size and thus may not fit into your new box.

3. Type **50** in the scale dialog box and click OK; the dialog box disappears and the lunch graphic shrinks down to 50% of its original size.

4. Select Object ➤ Scale. Note that the Scaling box reads 100%, as it did before. Any time you scale a graphic, its present size is always 100%, regardless of any scaling you have done before. Type **200**, and click OK. Now the lunch is twice the size it was.

5. Select Object ➤ Scale one more time, type **25**, and click OK. The lunch returns to its original size.

Remember that scaling a text box does not change the size of the type. If the box gets too small for the type size or content, type will be hidden outside the box.

Rotating an Object

The Rotate command on the Object menu is more precise than the Rotate tool on the toolbar. You'll remember from Chapter 2 that the Rotate tool allows you to grab an object and physically turn it. The Rotate menu command takes you one step further. It allows you to designate an exact angle of turn for objects and to turn them automatically. The Rotate menu offers you the option of rotating: Left 90°, Right 90°, or Other.

Let's make the word balloon at the right end of the banner come right out of the child's head by using the Rotate menu command.

1. Select the balloon.

2. Click on Object ➤ Rotate ➤ Other. The Rotate dialog box appears.

3. Click on the arrows to change 0 to 330, as shown here. The angle

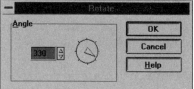

of rotation you've selected is indicated on the angle clock.

4. Click OK and the balloon readjusts to better align with the top of the child's head.

You'll notice that the text inside the word balloon does not rotate. It doesn't rotate because it's not word balloon text but instead a text block positioned over a square graphic (Thought Bubble B from the Accessories library). You can determine this in two ways:

◆ If you click once on the text, you'll see that it has its own handles. If you double-click on the text, the Edit Text dialog box will open with the text inside.

◆ If you click on the bubble, you'll discover that it has handles also.

Flipping Objects

The Flip command in the Object menu offers the same options as the Flip tool in the toolbar: Horizontal, Vertical, and Both. Refer to "Flipping Objects" in Chapter 2 for details.

Locking and Unlocking Objects

Once you have an object in the right position, you can lock it in place to keep it from moving around while you are working on other objects. A locked object will not move until you unlock it.

Now that we've got the bubble where we want it, let's lock it.

1. Select the bubble and from the Object menu, click on Lock. The handles on the bubble become smaller, indicating that it is locked.

2. To unlock the bubble, select it and click on Object ➤ Unlock (the menu option changes from Lock to Unlock when the selected item is already locked). The handles change back to their normal size to indicate that the object is not locked.

Aligning Objects

Aligning makes it easy to place two or more objects in exact relationship to each other. You can arrange the objects in eleven different ways:

Aligns objects by upper-left corners

Aligns objects by upper edges

Aligns objects by upper-right corners

Aligns objects by left edges

Aligns objects by centers, vertically and horizontally

Aligns objects by right edges

Aligns objects by lower-left corners

Aligns objects by lower edges

Aligns objects by lower-right corners

Aligns objects by centers, horizontally

Aligns objects by centers, vertically

Let's try aligning the headline School Open House with the classroom graphic in the banner.

1. Select both objects by clicking on one, holding down the Shift key, and then clicking on the other. Note how the two objects are positioned one above the other.

2. Select Object ➤ Align and the alignment options pop up, as outlined above.

3. Click on each of the options offered; as you click each one, its description appears in the lower portion of the screen.

4. Select the one that "aligns objects along vertical midlines" and click OK. The headline is now centered over the classroom graphic.

5. Once again, select Align from the Objects menu and choose "aligns objects by left edges." Click OK. The objects are now aligned at their left edges.

Aligning objects in this way is a faster and more accurate way to align your objects than trying to align them by sight alone. If you don't like the results of an alignment you've performed, remember you can always undo your action by clicking the Undo tool or choosing Edit ➤ Undo as long as you do it immediately.

◆ Using the Project Menu

The Project menu offers options for changing the basics of your project. The first two commands in the Project menu for all projects are always Change Backdrop and Change Layout. The other commands vary depending on the project type.

Changing the Backdrop

You can change the backdrop of your project at any time by clicking on Change Backdrop. If you have a backdrop already, a dialog box pops up letting you know that if you change the backdrop, you'll lose your current backdrop. If you have no backdrop (as is the case with our Open House banner), you go directly to the Backdrops Browser.

As usual, the backdrops available appear in the preview box as you click on them. If you decide not to add or change the backdrop, you can click on Cancel to return to the project unchanged.

 When you change a backdrop, all the layout elements remain the same and maintain the same position they had with the previous backdrop.

Let's try a few of the backdrops on the Open House banner.

1. Click on Project ➤ Change Backdrop.

2. Select Grad Pennant and click OK. The Grad Pennant appears underneath the banner, but it makes everything too confusing.

3. Select Edit ➤ Undo to change the banner back the way it was.

4. Click on Project ➤ Change Backdrop again.

 **5.** Select Hot Dog, shown here. This is certainly different, but not very appropriate.

6. Click Cancel.

 If you've experimented with several backdrops and you want to go back to having no backdrop at all, you won't be able to use the Undo command, since that only undoes your most recent action. But you can still return to a blank background by scrolling to the top of the list of graphics and selecting Blank Page.

Changing the Layout

As with Change Backdrop, when you click on Change Layout a dialog box pops up letting you know that if you change your layout, you'll lose your current layout. When you select a new layout, all objects in your project are deleted and replaced by the new layout.

Let's do a practice run without actually changing the layout of the banner.

1. Select Project ➤ Change Layout.

2. In the dialog box that appears, click on Yes.

3. The ready-made layout options appear in the Select a Layout dialog box. Click on a few of these layouts to see what they look like, but don't click on OK. You don't want to lose all your work.

4. When you're through looking at the layout options, click on Cancel. You will return to the project and no changes will have been made to the original layout.

Changing the Banner Length

When you're working on a banner, Banner Length is one of the command options on the Project menu. Clicking on Banner Length displays the dialog box shown here, which allows you to specify in inches where

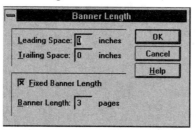

you want the length added: in front of the type (leading space) or behind it (trailing space).

The Fixed Banner Length option, which automatically adjusts the number of pages in the banner to fit the text, is selected by default. If you prefer, you can change the length manually by typing a number in the Banner Length box below. Right now, the Open House banner is set to print on three pages. Let's change it to five pages.

1. Click on Project ➤ Banner Length and type **5** in the Banner Length box. Do not change the leading or trailing spaces.

2. Click OK and the banner appears on five pages, as shown below (dotted lines appear between the pages). You can see that all we did was stretch the background, not any of the graphics on top.

Changing the banner length stretches the backdrop and any headlines that were part of the original layout but does not stretch any graphics on the banner or any headline added to the project. All these stay in essentially the same position as they were before the stretch. You'll need to grab handles and manually stretch graphics to fill the new space.

Let's look at another banner to see if it automatically adjusts.

1. Click on the File menu and select Open. At the prompt asking you if you want to save your work, click on No. We're done with Open House.

2. From the File Open dialog box, click on Show Ready Made Files, select the file called Room.brm, and click OK to open the file, shown below.

3. Select Project ➤ Banner Length.

4. Change the length to 5 pages and click OK. Everything on the banner stretches to fit five pages, as shown below. The reason the items on this banner stretch to fill five pages is that they are all either backdrop or headline, and backdrops and headlines stretch to fit the space available.

5. Now select Project ➤ Banner Length again, and this time change the leading space to 3 inches.

6. Click OK. The word *Francine* has been moved to the right 3 inches.

Browse through the ready-made banners and take a look at the variety of styles. Try changing the banner lengths and adjusting the leading and trailing spaces to see the effects.

Blending the Colors on a Page

Banners do not offer the Page Blend option, so you will not find it on the Project menu at the moment. The command does appear in almost every other project, however. With Page Blend, you can add texture to a page color by applying one of six different designs that blend the color in varying shadings.

Using Page Blend Alone

Let's take a look at Page Blend.

1. Pull down the File menu, select New, and click No when asked if you want to save the existing project.

2. Select Signs & Posters as your project, then choose Start From Scratch from the Select a Path dialog box, then Tall from the Sign Orientation dialog box, Blank Page from the Graphics Browser, and finally No Layout from the Select a Layout dialog box. You end up in the main project window with a blank piece of paper.

3. The Item Selector shows that Page is selected and the Color Selector indicates that the page color is white. Change the color by pulling down the Color Selector and choosing from the colors offered. Your page will become the color you selected.

4. Pull down the Item Selector and select Page Blend.

5. The default color for a page blend is black. Again pull down the Color Selector and change the color.

The page in your main project window does not change color because Page Blend is the secondary color and only shows up when you actually blend the colors using Page Blend from the Project Menu. Let's do that now.

6. Pull down the Project menu and select Page Blend. Solid is selected by default; this means that only the primary page color is in effect. Blend this color with the secondary page blend color by selecting Blend Across. The page changes, blending the two selected colors across the page as shown here.

7. Pull down the Project menu again and select Page Blend ➤ Blend Down. The page colors blend again, but in a different direction, as shown here. Continue through the list until you've seen all the blends.

Using Page Blend with a Backdrop

Let's try using Page Blend with a backdrop. First, choose one of the Page Blend options, choosing whatever colors you like. When your page is blended and colored just right, begin.

1. From the Project menu, select Change Backdrop.

2. From the Backdrops Browser, select Calendar. Your page now shows the Calendar graphic over the blended page.

3. Try some of the other backdrops and see how they work. You might want to change your page blend colors as well.

Some backdrops fill the entire page and when they do, you cannot see the page color at all. If the backdrop graphic is black in color, its color can be changed using the Item Selector and the Color Selector. Backdrop graphics that are multicolored can be lightened using the Shading Selector.

We'll cover this more in Part III, "Managing Graphics."

Choosing Other Project Commands

Other commands that are specific to particular projects appear on the Project menu. When you're working on a greeting card, for instance, options include Front of Card, Inside of Card, and Back of Card. Click on these to move among the different pages of the card. When you're working on a calendar, options include Change Month, Edit Day, Change Year and Calendar Options. These options change based on whether your calendar has a daily, weekly, monthly, or yearly format.

We'll cover the options specific to different types of projects in Chapter 5, "Understanding Print Shop Projects." For now, just know that you will find other commands on the Project menu than we've seen here when you're working on other projects.

◆ Using the View Menu

The View menu lets you change the way you view your project. Many of the commands in this menu are the same as those affiliated with the Zoom tool on the toolbar. The commands repeated here are Zoom In, Zoom Out, Fit to Window, 25%, 50%, Actual Size, 150%, and 200%. The result will be the same whether you select these commands from the Zoom tool or from the View menu. Refer to "Changing the View" in Chapter 2 for details.

The commands available only on the View menu are Hide Backdrop, Hide Placeholders, Hide Toolbar, and Hide Text Toolbar. If your screen is getting crowded, you may wish to hide one or more of these items to make a little more room. When an element is visible, the command on the View menu says Hide. When an element is hidden, the command changes to Show. For example, if you hide the toolbar, the command says Show Toolbar.

◆ Using the Extras Menu

Commands offered on the Extras menu include Smart Graphics, Custom Libraries, Select List Type, Edit Address List, Edit Custom List, Edit Return Address, and Export Graphics.

Using Smart Graphics

Smart Graphics allow you to create customized graphics, such as the stylized initial shown here, to use in your projects. Other Smart Graphics options include Numbers, Timepieces, and Borders. The Numbers option gives you the ability to customize numbers, much as the initial is customized. Timepieces allows you to customize a clock, choosing a graphic and time. And with Borders, you can create a border, mini-border or certificate border. You will learn more about all these in Chapter 7, "Creating Special Graphics."

Customizing Libraries

The Custom Libraries command allows you to merge and modify graphics libraries. See Chapter 6, "Working with Graphics Libraries," for a complete discussion of this command.

Accessing Lists

The Select List Type, Edit Address List, Edit Custom List, and Edit Return Address commands provide you with access to address and custom lists and let you merge these lists into your projects. This feature is particularly useful for signs, labels, mailing lists, and name tags. See Chapter 11, "Creating and Merging Lists" for more information.

Exporting Graphics

The Export Graphics command allows you to export graphics directly from the project window. (This command is also available in the Select a Project dialog box when you first open the program.) See Chapter 9, "Exporting Graphics," for information.

◆ Using the Help Menu

Print Shop Deluxe comes with an extensive Help library online. When in doubt, click on Help on the main menu bar and you'll be offered two options: Contents and Using Help. Using Help gives you specific instructions in the following topics: navigating in viewer, finding information, printing and copying, bookmarks and annotations, buttons and menus, and keyboard techniques. Contents takes you to the main Help screen, from which you can access the information you need directly or by performing a specific search. See Chapter 4, "Getting Help," for complete instructions.

◆ Endnotes

Mission accomplished. You now know everything you ever wanted to know about menus. You know:

- ◆ How to open, close, save, and print files

- ◆ How to choose your working preferences

- ◆ How to undo an edit or cut, copy, and paste objects

- ◆ How to duplicate everything in the project window or one object only

- ◆ How to add, edit, shadow, frame, move to the front, push to the back, flip, rotate, lock down, and align objects

- ◆ How to change a backdrop or a layout, adjust a banner length, and change the page blend or page color

- ◆ How to view the project in any size you like

- ◆ A bit about special projects filed under the Extras Menu

- ◆ Where to find Help when you need it

You're well on your way to mastering this program.

In Chapter 4, "Getting Help," we'll take a look at how to effectively use the online Help system in PSD Ensemble II.

Getting Help

Your mission: to understand Help, where to find it and how to use it

◆

In Chapter 3 you received a brief introduction to Help by way of the main menu. In this chapter, we'll explore all that Help has to offer: the various screens, dialog boxes, links, and other elements that help you find the information you need.

◆ Using the Main Help Screen

As you already know, you access the main Help screen, shown in Figure 4.1, by clicking on Help ➤ Contents. The left side of the screen lists five chapters designed to walk you through specifics of the program: The

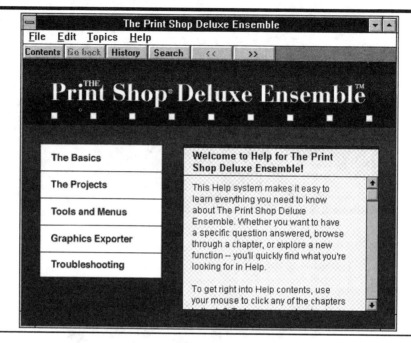

Figure 4.1:   Print Shop's main Help screen

Basics, The Projects, Tools and Menus, Graphics Exporter, and Trouble-shooting. You can click on any one of these to reach more specific information.

The right side of the Help screen contains some informative welcome text. If you scroll down through this text you'll see that some of the words are green, and some are green and underlined. This special text indicates a link to information on a related topic.

Help screens have three different linked elements—pop-up boxes, jumps, and notes. Whenever you move your cursor over one of these links, the cursor will change to a hand, indicating a link command. Green text is linked to a pop-up box that offers additional information about the current subject. Underlined green text is linked to a jump, which takes you directly to another Help screen. A note icon offers additional information on the current topic or a related topic when you click on it.

Using Links

Let's give it a try.

1. Select File ➤ New ➤ Banners ➤ Ready Made ➤ School ➤ School Open House to open the same Open House banner we used in Chapter 3.

2. In the main project window, click on Help, then on Contents. The Help screen appears.

3. Read through the welcome text. There are three jumps (green underlined text) in the welcome text: How to Access Help, Help Screen Links, and Using Help Commands. Click on How to Access Help, and the text box is filled with a brief explanation, telling you to click on a Help button if one appears or to click on the Help menu to access Help at any time.

4. At the top of the Help dialog box, click on the button labeled Go Back, and you return to the previous screen.

5. Click on Help Screen Links, and information on pop-ups, jumps, and notes appears. Read through it.

6. Click on Go Back again, then on Using Help Commands. Here you'll find an explanation of the buttons at the top of the Help dialog box, as follows:

Button	Action
Contents	Returns you to the initial Help screen
Go back	Returns you to the previous screen
History	Accesses a pop-up box that lists the last 40 Help screens you have used
Search	Calls up the Search dialog box, which allows you to search by word, phrase, or subject
<<	Moves you back one screen
>>	Moves you forward one screen

The left arrow button moves you between screens but does not necessarily return you to the last screen, since there are topics imbedded in screens. If you want to go to a previous screen, use Go Back.

7. Click on Go Back again to return to the initial Help screen.

Using the Help Chapters

Let's take a look now at the Help chapters.

1. Click on The Basics. A list of basics replaces the welcome informa-

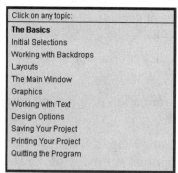

tion in the preview window on the right of the Help box, as shown here. You can select from this list to see information on a topic.

2. Click on The Basics in the preview area and a Help screen entitled The Basics appears. Here you find a brief introduction followed by the same list you saw in the initial Help screen. Note that the list is in green underlined type, indicating jumps.

3. Click on Initial Selections and you jump to that screen. Note that this screen also has jumps.

4. Click on the Contents button at the top of the screen to return to the initial Help screen.

You can continue your search for help in this way by clicking through the other chapter options, or you can search for help on a specific subject, as described in "Searching Help" later in the chapter.

Using Keyboard Shortcuts

In addition to links, pop-ups, notes, buttons, lists, menus, and chapters, the Help system also lets you use keyboard shortcuts to access the information you need, as follows:

Key(s)	Action
Ctrl+C, Ctrl+Ins	Copies the displayed topic to the Clipboard
Ctrl+Shift+Alt+F1	Jumps to the Contents screen
Ctrl+Shift+Alt+F3	Takes you to the last topic viewed (Go Back)
Ctrl+Shift+Alt+F4	Brings up the History list
Ctrl+Shift+Alt+F5	Displays the previous topic in the browse sequence
Ctrl+Shift+Alt+F6	Displays the next topic in the browse sequence
Tab	Moves to next jump
Shift+Tab	Moves to previous jump
Ctrl+Tab	Highlights all jumps
Esc	Removes the topmost pop-up
Alt	Removes all pop-ups

◆ Searching Help

You can narrow your search criteria by using the Search dialog box, shown below, which is accessed by clicking on the Search button at the top of the initial Help screen. Your cursor will appear in the Search by Word text box. If you click on the arrow next to this box, you'll see a drop-down list of your most recent searches. You can select one of these or type a word, phrase, or subject to search by in the Search by Word box. The Search dialog box also has options for searching in all topic groups, selected topic groups (indicated just to the right), or the current topic only.

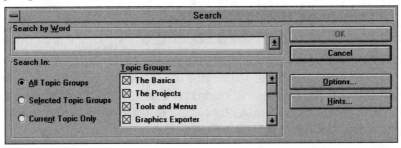

Let's search for help on backdrops.

1. In the main Help screen, click on the Search button. Type **backdrops**.

2. Click on the Selected Topic Groups option and then check The Projects.

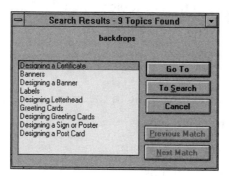

3. Click on OK. The Search Results dialog box appears with a list of nine topics, as shown here. The topics are listed according to how many times the search word appears in each, so the search word *backdrops* appears most often in the Designing a Certificate library file and least often in the Designing a Post Card file.

4. Select Banners and click on Go To.

5. The Help screen opens below the Search Results dialog box. Click on Cancel to go to the Banners file. You'll note that this Help file includes a graphic and various jump commands that take you to other relevant Help files if you click on them.

6. Click on Contents to return to the initial Help menu.

To fine-tune a search, you can click on the Options button in the Search dialog box to bring up the Search Options dialog box, shown here, and

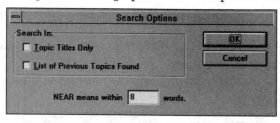

designate that the search take place in topic titles only or in the list of previous topics found. You can also change the number in the section that says "NEAR means within 8 words." It searches for two words that appear in the same Help screen within a certain number of words of each other. For example, you can specify a word search where the word *bee* and the word *honey* must appear within six words of each other by typing **6** in the box. When you've made your selections, click on OK to return to the Search dialog box.

Depending on how you want a search conducted, you can type different parameters in the Search by Word section of the Search dialog box. You can get an overview of search parameters by clicking on the Hints button. All the search variations are illustrated for you there. For example, the following list shows how you can designate the bee search in different ways:

Text	Result
Bee	Look for the word bee
"Bees love honey"	Look for this exact quote
Bee*	Look for words that begin with bee
Bee and honey	Look for both words together
Bee or honey	Look for either word
Bee near honey	Look for bee within a certain number of words (the default is 8) of honey
Bee not honey	Look for bee when honey is not present
Bee not (honey or hive)	Look for bee when neither honey nor hive is present

◆ Using the Help Menu Bar

The Help menu bar offers additional options for searching, including menus for File, Edit, Topics, and Help. Let's take a look at each one.

Using the File Menu

The File menu offers options including Print Topic, Print Setup, and Exit. Print Topic prints whatever appears on your Help screen. Print Setup sets up your printer before printing. Exit exits Help.

Using the Edit Menu

The Edit menu offers various ways to copy or mark Help text: Copy, Annotate, Place a Bookmark, and Jump to a Bookmark. Let's work our way through these.

1. Click on the Search button. The Search dialog box appears. Click on the arrow to the right of the Search by Word box and choose *backdrops* from the top of the list of recent searches.

2. Click OK and again you are presented with nine topics on the Search Results dialog box.

3. Click on Banners ➤ Go To ➤ Cancel to reach the Banners Help screen.

4. Select Edit ➤ Copy to save the entire screen (without the graphic) in the Clipboard. This information will remain in the Clipboard until it is replaced by new information from another copy command. You can paste this Help topic into any word processing program, or you can paste it into an annotation. We'll choose the annotation route.

5. Click on Edit ➤ Annotate. The Annotate dialog box pops up, as

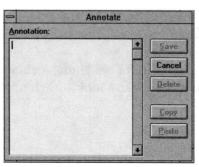

shown here. You can use this dialog box to add your own comments to Help or to create your own links from one Help screen to another.

6. Click on Paste; all the text you just copied into the Clipboard is pasted into the Annotate dialog box. (If you wanted to, you could just type your own note in the box.)

7. Click on Save. You return to the Banners Help screen with a paper clip showing at the beginning of the screen. This lets you know that you have created a note here.

8. Click on the paper clip to access the note. The Annotate dialog box appears again with the note in place.

9. Click on Delete; the annotation and the paper clip disappear.

This is a great way to create reminders for yourself about new ways you have devised to make the program work more efficiently for you.

Another useful Help technique is to mark a particularly helpful screen with a bookmark so that you can find it again easily.

10. You should still be in the Banners Help screen. If you're not, follow steps 1–3 above to get there. Once the screen is open, select Edit ➤ Place a Bookmark.

11. The Bookmark Define dialog box, shown here, opens with the

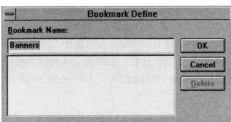

current Help screen in the Bookmark Name box. You can click on OK to leave this as the name of the bookmark or you can type another name first. For this example, leave it at Banners and click on OK.

The Bookmark define dialog box disappears and you're back in the Banners Help screen. Even though there is no visual indication, you have placed a bookmark on this page.

12. Click on Go Back to return the initial Help screen.

13. Click on Edit ➤ Jump to a Bookmark, and all your bookmarks are listed.

14. Select Banners (it will be selected by default if that is the only bookmark you have) and click on the Go To button to jump immediately to the Banners Help screen.

To delete a bookmark, you can click on Edit ➤ Place a Bookmark, select the bookmark you want to delete, and click on Delete.

Using the Topics Menu

The Topics menu is a duplication of the main chapters listed on the left side of the initial Help screen. Click on any one of the topics to see all the different Help options offered.

Using the Help Menu

The Help menu options are Help Contents and About Viewer. About Viewer is authoring information. Help Contents gives you access to a library devoted to helping you learn how to use Help. This special how-to library is the same one accessed from the main project window by choosing Help ➤ Using Help and is covered in the next section of this chapter.

15. Select File ➤ Exit to return to the main project window.

◆ Accessing the Using Help Library

For complete instructions on how to use Print Shop's Help library, choose Help ➤ Using Help from the main project window. The topics covered by the library are too numerous to cover in detail here, but they are easily accessible via a series of buttons and lists as follows:

Button	Topic	Subtopics
	Navigating in Viewer	Navigating through Your Title Using Links Browsing through Topic Sequences Jumping to the Table of Contents Returning to the Last Topic Viewed Returning to Any Topic Viewed
	Finding Information	Using Full-Text Search Browsing through the Search Results Using Search Operators Using Multiple Search Operators

Printing and Copying

Printing and Copying Information in Your Title
Changing Printers and Printer Options
Printing Topics
Copying Topic Text

 Bookmarks and Annotations

Annotating Your Title
Using Bookmarks
Jumping to a Bookmark
Annotating a Topic
Viewing an Annotation
Copying and Pasting Annotations

 Buttons and Menus

File Menu Commands
Edit Menu Commands
Topics Menu Options
Help Menu Commands
Using the Button Bar

 Keyboard Techniques

◆ Finding Help in Dialog Boxes

You can get instant help from many dialog boxes by clicking on their Help buttons. The Help system is context-sensitive, so a click on a Help button in a dialog box will take you instantly to a Help screen on that particular subject.

Let's try it.

1. You should still have the Open House banner open. Double-click on the headline.

2. The Headline dialog box appears. Click on the Help button. A Help screen entitled *Entering and Editing Headline Text* pops up.

That's all there is to it.

◆ Endnotes

Now you'll never be at a loss if you need help. You know how to:

◆ Access the main help screen and the special Using Help library

◆ Use Help's main topics, links, buttons, and menu bar to access the information you need

◆ Navigate through the Help screens quickly with keyboard shortcuts

◆ Search for help on specific words, phrases, or subjects

◆ Get context-sensitive help from any dialog box

Now that you've learned how to use Print Shop's toolbar, menus, and Help system, we'll take a closer look at the individual projects Print Shop offers in Chapter 5, "Understanding Print Shop Projects."

Understanding Print Shop Projects

Your mission: to maximize your knowledge of the Print Shop projects

◆

This is your introduction to the eleven great projects you can create with Print Shop:

- ◆ Greeting Cards
- ◆ Letterhead
- ◆ Calendars
- ◆ Signs & Posters
- ◆ Envelopes
- ◆ Labels
- ◆ Banners
- ◆ Postcards
- ◆ Certificates
- ◆ Business Cards

All are different and yet all share common design steps that lead to a creative conclusion. In this chapter, we'll explore the design elements that are unique to individual projects. But first, let's review the common design elements.

◆ Common Design Elements

PSD Ensemble II simplifies the creative process. Many of the steps and most of the design elements available in Print Shop are common for all projects. The first step, of course, is to select which type of project you want to work on. Next, you must select a path.

Selecting a Path

You'll recall from Chapter 1 that whether you're creating a greeting card, a business card, or any other project, the first step after choosing the project is to decide if you will create the project using ready-made design selections or if you will start from scratch.

Starting with a Ready-Made Project

A ready-made project may include backdrops, text, headlines, graphics… in other words, any of the available design elements, combined to create a project. The term *ready-made* is a little deceiving. While they are complete projects that can be printed as they are, this does not mean that you must keep the exact design as it's presented. Another way to look at ready-made projects is as a group of design elements created to get you started, then to be changed and modified to suit your own creative vision.

You can make modifications to almost all of the individual elements that make up a particular ready-made design, as we did with the Open House banner in Chapter 3 and the Car Wash sign in Chapter 2. We say *almost all* because some elements are locked and cannot be changed. (See "Locking and Unlocking Objects" in Chapter 3 for an explanation of locked objects.)

Some ready-made projects have other projects coordinated to match. For example, a greeting card may have a coordinating envelope or banner.

Let's take a look at a greeting card with a coordinating envelope.

1. In the Select a Project dialog box, select Greeting Cards ➤ Ready Made ➤ Celebration.

itsaboy.grm
This project has a coordinating Envelope.

2. Click on It's a Boy! to preview it. Below the preview, shown here, there is a note indicating that it has a coordinating envelope.

3. Click on Cancel three times to return to the Select a Project dialog box.

4. Select Stationery ➤ Ready Made ➤ Envelope.

itsaboy.erm
This project has a coordinating Greeting Card.

5. From the list, select It's a Boy! and the coordinating envelope appears in the preview window, as shown here.

Coordinating projects are available for virtually all projects and always have the same name from one project to the next to make them easy to locate.

Starting from Scratch

When you start from scratch, it is up to you to choose every aspect of the design. The next few sections of this chapter deal specifically with the choices offered when you elect to start from scratch.

Choosing an Orientation

When you select Start From Scratch from the Select a Path dialog box, the next screen will ask you to select an orientation for your project. Orientation refers to how the design elements will initially be laid out.

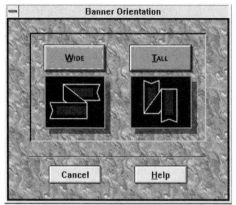

For example, if you are creating a banner, your selections are Wide or Tall, as shown here.

You will have to choose an orientation for any project you create from scratch, although the arrangement of the elements will change depending on the project selection. For example, if you've chosen stationery as your project, you'll be asked if you are designing letterhead, envelopes, postcards, notepads, or business cards. Each requires a different orientation decision, yet all contain common design elements, which is especially useful when you're trying to maintain a consistent look for business or family projects.

Browsing for a Backdrop

After you've selected the appropriate orientation, you will be prompted to select a backdrop. The exception to this rule is label projects, which do not have backdrops due to their size.

The Backdrops Browser defaults to PSD Backdrops, showing you those backdrops that fit the orientation of your current project. You can expand your backdrop choices by changing the selections to All Libraries or to a library that sounds like it might better suit your requirements, such as Business Backdrops.

You may also want to use the Search utility to see if there's a specific theme backdrop that fits your design. Figure 5.1, for instance, shows the Backdrops Browser for a wide backdrop after a search on the keyword *sports*. (See Chapter 1 for complete search instructions.)

When you select the Search Tall and Wide Backdrops option, the graphic will automatically adjust to your current page size. In other words, if you're working on a wide page format and the chosen backdrop was designed for a tall page format, the graphic will resize itself to fit in the wide format.

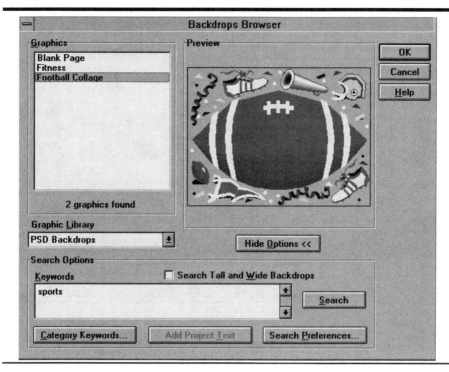

Figure 5.1:   A search on the keyword *sports* in PSD Backdrops finds only
two backdrops.

This might create backdrops that look stretched or squished, but in most
cases, the graphics work just fine. You, of course, will be the judge of
whether it works for your project.

Selecting a Layout

After you've selected your backdrop, you will be asked to select a layout.
A layout is a variety of shapes and sizes of placeholders for headlines, text,
graphics, and other objects that may be included in your design. The layouts offered in the Select a Layout dialog box, shown in Figure 5.2, are
designed to creatively maximize the page surface of the project. PSD
Ensemble II gives you the option of selecting a layout and then adding
additional placeholders or modifying or deleting placeholders from the
selected layout once you reach the main project window.

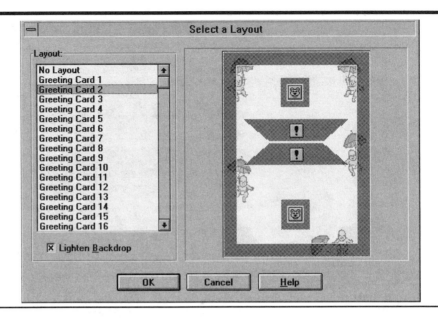

Figure 5.2:   The Select a Layout dialog box offers a wide variety of layouts to choose from, or you can click on No Layout and create your own.

A larger selection of predesigned layouts is available if you check the Lighten Backdrop box. This makes the backdrop less dominant so it's possible to put more graphics or text over it without looking too busy.

Now that you've taken care of the preliminary design issues, it's time to proceed to the precise details of your project's design. In the sections ahead, we'll describe those elements that are unique to each project in PSD Ensemble II.

◆ Project-Specific Design Elements

The design elements available to you in Print Shop will vary depending on the type of project you undertake. Let's take a look at each type of project now.

Designing Greeting Cards

You can create unique greeting cards for invitations, announcements or special occasions, choosing from an array of graphics and text options and styles. Greeting cards come in four different orientations: side-fold, side-fold spread, top-fold, and top-fold spread. Spread-type cards let you fill the entire area inside the card. Non-spread cards let you use only half of the inside of the card.

When you go through the initial steps of choosing a backdrop and layout for a greeting card, you are choosing these elements for the front of the card only. When you move to the inside of the card for the first time, you are prompted to select a backdrop and layout for this part of the card. And when you navigate to the back of the card for the first time, you are again prompted to select a layout (backdrops are not available for the back of a greeting card).

 Greeting cards and postcards (discussed under "Designing Stationery" later in the chapter) are the only multipage projects in Print Shop. To move from page to page in these projects, you use the Navigation tool. (See Chapter 1 for more information about the Navigation tool.)

Let's take a look at some greeting-card-specific design elements.

1. Open the ready-made birthday card called Frog Birthday. (To do so, select File ➤ New ➤ Greeting Cards ➤ Ready Made ➤ Celebration ➤ Frog Birthday ➤ Select.)

2. Click on the Project menu. Note the options to go to the front of the card (you are already there, so this one is checked), the inside of card, or the back of card. These Project menu commands duplicate the Navigation tool.

3. Select Inside of Card. Inside, you can see that this is a side-fold spread card with no backdrop, only a colored page.

4. Click on Project ➤ Change Backdrop. The Backdrops Browser dialog box opens. Note that you have 49 backdrop graphics available.

5. Click on the arrow next to Graphic Library and change the selection to All Libraries. Now you have 87 backdrops available.

6. Click on the Search Options button and select the Search Tall and Wide Backdrops box.

7. Click on Search. Now you have 377 backdrops available. (Remember, you're filling a wide space in the side-fold spread card, so tall backdrops will be stretched to fit.)

8. Select Bon Voyage from the list of backdrops. This is the same backdrop you used in Chapter 1 for the front of the party invitation. Notice how it is elongated to fit the spread area, as shown here.

9. Click on OK to return to the main project window.

10. Click on the Navigation tool to go to the back of the card.

11. Click on Project and note that the Change Backdrop option is not available for the back of the card. Many people use the back of a greeting card to give themselves credit for designing such a great card.

Here's an idea: create a miniature coloring book for someone special using the greeting card project. Fill the four pages of the greeting card with graphics, add a headline personalizing the "book," and then print the project in coloring book format (see "Printing a Project" in Chapter 3 for instructions).

Designing Signs and Posters

When you choose Signs & Posters from the Select a Project dialog box, you can make a whole array of different projects. Yes, you can make a sign or poster for a garage sale, car wash, school dance, or notice of hours, but you can also make bookmarks, gift wrap, bumper stickers, and more.

Let's look at three great projects. We'll start with a bumper sticker.

1. Select File ➤ New ➤ Signs & Posters ➤ Start From Scratch. Next, hold down the Ctrl key and select Wide for the orientation. You are taken to a wide, blank page in the main project window.

2. Select Object ➤ Add ➤ Mini-border. A mini-border placeholder appears on the page.

3. Double-click on the mini-border, choose All Libraries, select Memo Planes, and click on OK.

4. Move and resize the mini-border to fit into the lower half of the page (see "Moving and Resizing Objects" in Chapter 2 for instructions). Leave the top half of the page blank.

5. Select Object ➤ Add ➤ Square Graphic. A square graphic placeholder appears on the page.

6. Move the graphic placeholder inside the mini-border on the left.

7. Add a second square graphic placeholder in the same way, only this time place it on the right inside the mini-border.

8. Double-click on the placeholder on the left, choose All Libraries, select Eagle, and click on OK. An eagle appears inside the mini-border on the left.

9. Double-click on the right placeholder, choose All Libraries, select Turkey, and click on OK. A turkey appears inside the mini-border on the right.

10. Adjust the two graphics to make them fit neatly inside the mini-border, the eagle all the way to the left and the turkey all the way to the right.

11. Select Object ➤ Add ➤ Text. A text placeholder appears in the project.

12. Double-click on the placeholder and type **How can I soar with Eagles when I work with Turkeys?** in the Edit Text dialog box. Select a text color and style, then click on OK to place the text in the project.

13. Move and resize the headline to fill the area inside the mini-border between the two graphics.

14. You should now have a completed bumper sticker filling half of your project page. Click on Edit ➤ Select All to select all the items in the project.

15. Click on Edit ➤ Duplicate. The bumper sticker is duplicated.

16. Move the duplicate copy to fill the upper half of the project page, so you have a page with two bumper stickers as shown here.

17. Print the project on full-page peel-off paper and cut it in half to create two bumper stickers.

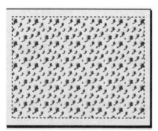

You can also make a sheet of gift wrapping paper by using a backdrop with repeating elements such as lips or red balloons, as shown here. The limitation on this idea is the size of paper your printer will accept, which will generally be regular letter size.

Bookmarks are a good project; you can create just one or a whole pageful, as shown here. Select the tall orientation, stretch (resize) any graphic (column and row graphics work particularly well), and then use the duplicate option to create a pageful. You can print your bookmarks directly on card-stock paper or print them on regular paper and photocopy them onto card-stock.

Designing Banners

Banners are great for announcing a grand opening or a special sale, a school dance or a new recycling program. Banners can be coordinated to match a party invitation or an announcement or a sale flyer by using the same graphic elements in both projects.

Unlike most other projects, banners require you to select a layout (you cannot skip over the Select a Layout dialog box). Once you've chosen a layout for a banner, you'll find that some of its design elements cannot be changed because the placeholders are locked. Locked objects cannot be moved or resized, but some can be deleted. As previously mentioned, the locked elements have smaller handles than unlocked ones, allowing you to identify them easily.

Banners can be wide (horizontal) or tall (vertical). You can change the length of either of these to print on 3 to 35 pages (only 6 pages will be readable in preview). To change the length, click on Project ➤ Banner Length (the only extra command in the Project menu for banners) and type a new number of pages in the Banner Length dialog box. Here you can also change the position of the message on a banner by adjusting the leading space before the message begins and the trailing space after the message. If you add more space to either of these dimensions, it will move the graphic further away from the edges. (These techniques are discussed in "Changing the Banner Length" in Chapter 3.)

You add text to a banner by double-clicking on a banner text box to reach the Banner dialog box, shown here. This dialog box looks similar

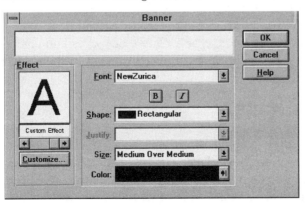

to the Headline dialog box, but keep in mind that banner text boxes do not behave the same as headline boxes. Unless you resize it manually, a headline box remains the same size no matter how much text you put in it; the text inside spreads or shrinks to fill the box. A banner text box, on the other hand, grows larger as you add text, increasing the length of the banner. You can type a total of 63 characters into the box at the top of the Banner dialog box.

The Banner dialog box shown above is for a horizontal banner. Horizontal banners can have one or two lines of text, and you can choose from various font, style, shape, justification, size, color, and custom effect options. (Vertical banners do not offer shape, justification, or size options due to the orientation of the text on the page.) The Size option lets you designate the size of one line of banner text as it relates to the other (if any), as follows:

Single Line

Small Over Large

Large Over Small

Medium Over Medium

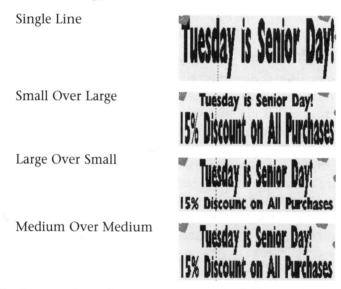

If the layout of your banner contains a locked text placeholder but you do not wish to add text to it, double-click on the placeholder, and in the Edit Text dialog box that appears, type a couple of spaces and click OK. The text placeholder will disappear with no text added to the project.

Designing Certificates

Certificates are a great way to recognize a special achievement for the highest sales, the most improved player, the highest grades, or the greatest Mom or Dad. The certificate project category has many creative options. For instance, you can make a plain piece of white paper look like an expensive piece of watermarked parchment. Let's give this a try.

1. Select File ➤ New ➤ Certificates ➤ Start From Scratch ➤ Wide ➤

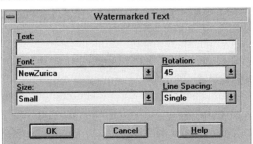

Watermarked Text. The Watermarked Text dialog box, shown here, prompts you to enter the text you'd like to use.

2. Type your text. Initials are a good choice. Customize the text, selecting its color, size, orientation, and font.

3. Click on OK and the watermarked text is previewed in Backdrops Browser. The default is to screen the color to 10%. You can experi-

ment with this in the main project window using the Color and Shading Selectors. In the example shown here we've made the watermark text white and the page color light gray to make the watermark stand out more.

If you would like to use watermarked paper in a project other than a certificate, you can. Just start a certificate project, create your watermarked paper, and go to the main project window with no other objects added. Save the project as a TIFF or WMF file, and you can import this TIFF or WMF into any other project and size it to fit the area you want watermarked, either part or all of the page.

Because most certificates are signed, you can add signature blocks for a number of signers in different layouts. Two more items that certificates generally have are a place for the recipient's name and an official seal. All of these elements can be added by clicking on Object ➤ Add and then making your selection from the drop-down menu, as described in "Adding Objects" in Chapter 3. See Chapter 10 for instructions on adding signature blocks and Chapter 7 for designing seals.

When there are a number of awards to prepare, the names in the title block can be changed from one recipient to another automatically by using the Name List option (more on this in Chapter 11, "Creating and Merging Lists").

Designing Stationery

Under the Stationery category, you can create single-page or notepad letterheads, envelopes in two sizes, postcards, or business cards.

Selecting ready-made stationery gives you an added bonus: coordinating projects. As noted above, ready-made letterheads may have coordinating envelopes, business cards, or postcards. Some even have coordinated labels. See "Starting with a Ready-Made Project" near the beginning of this chapter for instructions.

You can create coordinated stationery of your own design by selecting the same graphics and text options when you design the letterhead as when you design the envelope. (An even easier way is to copy and paste graphics and text boxes from one project to another.) The secret to coordinating projects is to save them the right way. Here's an example.

1. Once you have the coordinating projects completed, select File ➤ Save As. The File Save As dialog box appears.

2. Click on the Options button and type a description in the Save Options dialog box. For example, if you are saving the letterhead for a coordinating letterhead and envelope set, type **coordinating envelope** in the Description area. For the envelope, type **coordinating letterhead**. That way when you open either of these files, your description will appear below the project as it is previewed and you'll know that there is a matching project you can access as well.

3. When you save the coordinated letterhead and envelope, give them the same name. They will automatically be given different extensions (.pdl for the letterhead and .pce for the envelope).

Some letterhead and notepad layouts contain a large text block that allows you to type a letter or note to be printed as part of the project. (You can always add this text block if it is not a part of the layout.) Keep in mind that notepads are half the size of a regular piece of paper and automatically print two to a page.

Another stationery project is postcards. As with greeting cards, Print Shop's other multipage project, you use the Navigation tool to move from page to page, but postcards have only two pages, while greeting cards have four. Postcards are great as customer contact cards, informal invitations, moving notifications, or special announcements.

When you print a postcard, you will need to feed the paper into your printer twice, once to print the front of the card and once to print the back. You can purchase postcard paper stock for your printer to print on. (All Print Shop postcards are 4¼" by 5½".) Let's take a look at the special print options you'll see for postcards.

1. Select File ➤ New ➤ Stationery ➤ Ready Made ➤ Post Cards. Open whichever ready-made postcard you like and click on File ➤ Print. The Print dialog box pops up, as shown here.

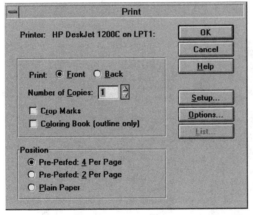

2. Look at the Position options at the bottom of the dialog box—Pre-Perfed: 4 per page, Pre-Perfed: 2 per page, and Plain Paper. Here you can designate whether you want to print two or four postcards on a page of pre-perfed (pre-perforated) postcard paper or to print on plain paper.

3. Check the Crop Marks option if you're printing on plain paper. This will give you guidelines of where to cut the paper to separate the postcards. You won't need crop marks with perforated card paper.

4. Select either Front or Back to indicate which side you're printing, and click on OK to start printing.

One other interesting postcard option is to select a postcard layout that is approved by the U.S. Postal Service. (Just choose USPS Layouts at the layout stage.) You can also designate a return address to appear on all postcards that you create. See Chapter 11, "Creating and Merging Lists," for details about both of these options.

Designing Calendars

You can create a calendar that reflects your style, your business, or your goals using the Calendar option. Whether they are ready-made or created from scratch, you can personalize calendars with your own chosen graphics, notes, and red-letter days.

Calendars can be yearly, monthly, weekly, or daily, as shown in Figure 5.3.

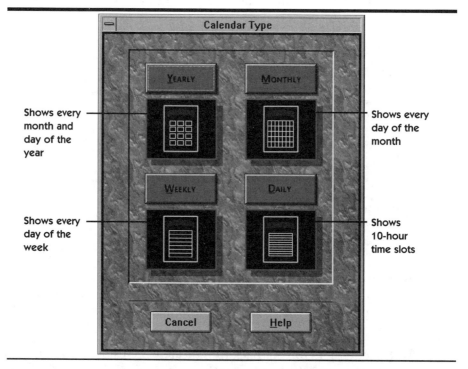

Figure 5.3:   Choose a yearly, monthly, weekly, or daily calendar.

If you select Yearly, you'll be prompted to choose a calendar year. If you select Monthly, you'll be asked to choose a month and year. If you select Weekly, you'll need to choose a week, month, the year, and the starting date. You can specify any day as the beginning of your week. For instance, you can begin your weekly calendar on Thursday instead of Sunday if you like. And finally, if you choose Daily, you will be prompted to select the day, month, year, and time period for the calendar. You can choose any 10-hour period using either a 12- or a 24-hour clock.

Let's create a daily calendar and see what calendar-specific options are available in the main project window.

1. Select File ➤ New ➤ Calendars ➤ Start From Scratch ➤ Daily.

2. Complete the Calendar Day dialog box as shown here. Choose October 1995, then click on 13 (a Friday) for the date. Select the 12-hour clock option and choose 8:00 AM to 5:00 PM for the time frame.

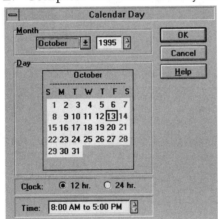

3. Select the orientation, backdrop, and layout of your choice in the dialog boxes that appear next. As with banners, you must select a layout for a calendar.

4. In the main project window, click on the Project menu and you'll see three commands specific to calendars. When working with a daily calendar, these commands are Edit Hour, Change Day, and Calendar Options.

5. Click on Edit Hour and the Edit Hour dialog box pops up, as shown in Figure 5.4.

To add text to an hour of the calendar, click on that hour, then on the Edit Text button. A text box will appear in which you can type your note. When you're done, click on OK. To add a graphic, click on an hour, then on the Select Graphic button. The Graphics Browser appears, from which you can select the graphic to include. Click on OK to place the

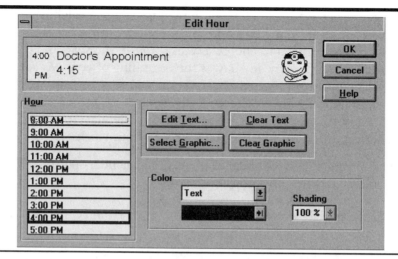

Figure 5.4: You can add graphics, text, and design elements to a daily calendar in the Edit Hour dialog box.

graphic in the hour. You can also double-click on the text or graphics placeholder at the top of the dialog box to reach the text box or the Graphics Browser, respectively.

6. Make your graphic and text selections and click OK to return to the main project window.

7. Click on Project ➤ Change Day. The Calendar Day dialog box reappears so you can change the day if you like. Click on cancel to return to the main project window.

8. Select Project ➤ Calendar Options and the Daily Calendar Options

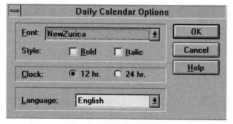

dialog box pops up, as shown here. Here you can select the font and text style, change the type of clock, and choose a language: English, French, Spanish, German, or Italian.

9. Click on OK to return to the main project window, then select the calendar box that contains the calendar lines.

10. Now click on the Item Selector and you'll note that there are three calendar-specific options—Calendar Lines, Behind Calendar, and Calendar Text.

11. Click on Calendar Lines and change the color of the lines using the Color Selector (see "Coloring and Shading an Area" in Chapter 2 for instructions). You can change the color behind the calendar or the color of the calendar text in the same way.

When you're working on a weekly, monthly, or yearly calendar, the Project commands are similar to the options for a daily calendar, with slight variations. For instance, the Edit Day command for a weekly or monthly calendar offers options that are similar to those offered by the Edit Hour command for a daily calendar. (Yearly calendars do not have either command.)

When you click on Project ➤ Calendar Options for a weekly calendar, you will be offered the same choices as with daily calendars. The calendar options for monthly and yearly calendars are a bit different.

The Monthly Calendar Options dialog box includes three extra options: Month Thumbnails (shown here), which places thumbnails of the pre- ceding and following months at the bottom of your calendar; Preceding/Following Days, which includes the ending days of the preceding month and the beginning days of the following month on your calendar, as space allows; and Red Sundays, which prints Sundays in red. The Yearly Calendar Options dialog box offers the same Red Sundays option and lets you choose whether you want the month blocks to appear plain, underlined, or boxed in your calendar.

Designing Labels

With Print Shop Deluxe Ensemble II you can create custom labels for letters, packages, video and audio tapes, computer disks, file folders, or anything else. Labels can be designed to print on a variety of label shapes and, of course, print multiple copies per page.

First, let's look at a ready-made label.

1. Select File ➤ New ➤ Labels ➤ Ready Made. Choose whichever ready-made label you like.

2. In the main project window, click on File ➤ Print. (A note may pop up telling you that the label text will be scaled down to 99% of its original size in order to fit on the label. If you see this note, just click on OK.)

3. The Print dialog box, shown here, pops up. Note that the number

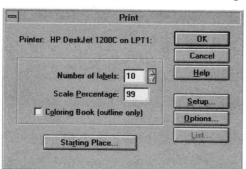

of labels to be printed is already set (in this case, it's set to 10). This is the number of labels that will fit on a page, given the size of the chosen label.

4. Click on the Starting Place button at the bottom of the dialog box. The Starting Place dialog box, shown here, pops up. This is the layout of your label page. You can click on any of the label squares to designate where you want to begin printing your labels. This is particularly useful if you are not using an entire sheet of labels. Note when you return to the Print dialog box that the number of copies you'll be printing changes to match your starting place selection.

Now let's design a label from scratch.

1. Select File ➤ New ➤ Labels ➤ Start From Scratch.

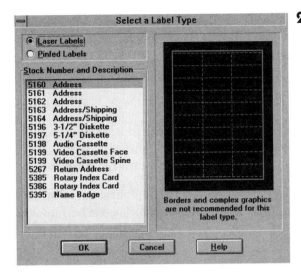

2. The Select a Label Type dialog box, shown here, pops up. At the top of the dialog box, you can choose between laser or pinfed labels. (The default is laser labels.) Select the label type appropriate for your printer and click through the list of labels to see the different types displayed in the preview area to the right.

3. Select a label type and click on OK to go directly to the Select a Layout dialog box. Since labels are small and usually text-intensive, backdrops are not available for labels.

4. Select a layout and click on OK to move to the main project window. From here on your options will be the same as with ready-made labels.

◆ One Last Tip

There will come a time when you want to cover up part of an object in a project, maybe a portion of a locked graphic or a border that interferes with something else on your project. When this happens:

1. In the main project window, click on Object ➤ Add ➤ Text.

2. Double-click on the text placeholder.

3. In the Edit Text dialog box, hit the spacebar once or twice instead of typing any text.

4. Click on OK.

5. You'll return to the main project window with a blank text block. Click on it.

6. From the Item Selector, select Behind Text, then change the color to white (or whatever color the page or object you want to hide is) using the Color Selector.

7. With the text block still selected, click on Object ➤ Order ➤ Bring to Front.

You end up with a text block that has nothing in it. (You'll only be able to see it when you select it, showing its handles.) You can place this empty text block over any object or piece of an object on the project to hide it.

This idea is an example of how you can create your own solutions to problems and make the Print Shop program work even better for you.

◆ Endnotes

You now know the projects, their common design elements, and their project-specific design elements. You also know:

◆ That the basic design options are the same from project to project but that some commands are unique to certain projects

◆ How to lighten a backdrop to increase your layout options

◆ How to create a personal coloring book or special wrapping paper

◆ How many characters you can type into a banner text block

◆ How to create coordinating letterhead, envelopes, and labels, then save them so you can locate them easily

◆ When to add crop marks to a printout of a postcard

◆ How to watermark a page and copy that page into another project if you want

◆ How to pick a day on a calendar, make a note about a meeting, and add a graphic

◆ How to print a series of labels, starting where you designate on the sheet of labels

In Part II, "Managing Graphics," we'll take an in-depth look at graphics, including graphics libraries, special graphics, and exporting and importing graphics.

Part Two:

Managing Graphics

ANNOUNCING

CHAPTER SIX

Working with Graphics Libraries

Your mission: to learn to navigate Print Shop's graphics libraries and to create and modify your own custom libraries

◆

Print Shop Deluxe Ensemble II has possibly the most comprehensive graphics library of any desktop publishing program available today. With some 4,500 graphics, there's bound to be more than one graphic that not only fills your creative needs for a project but offers you new ideas that expand your creative vision. This great diversity is made even better by the added ability to search the libraries and to create your own custom libraries.

More than 80 graphics libraries offer you images in a variety of sizes and on a wide range of subject matters. There are so many graphics in this program it's unlikely you'll ever see all of them unless you go exploring. If you do, make sure you note the location of graphics you find interesting so you can make a custom library of all your favorites later.

The mere size of the available libraries makes it absolutely critical that you know how to get around in this graphics world quickly and efficiently. Let's look at the structure of the libraries so we can negotiate through the graphics maze.

◆ Types of Graphics

There are three main types of graphics stored in libraries: backdrops, layouts, and graphics. Of these three, you will have direct access to only two in a library format: backdrops and graphics. Layouts are available only from the Select a Layout dialog box.

◆ Backdrop libraries are opened with the Backdrops Browser, which appears automatically when you create a project from scratch, or when you select Change Backdrop from the Project menu of an open project. Mini-backdrops are available from the Graphics Browser, which appears when you double-click on a graphic.

◆ Layout libraries are opened using the Select a Layout dialog box, which appears automatically when you create a project from scratch, or when you select Change Layout from the Project menu of an open project.

◆ Graphics libraries are opened from the Graphics Browser, which appears when you double-click on a placeholder or an existing graphic or when you add a graphic.

Graphics libraries are divided into graphic shapes: squares, columns, rows, ruled lines, mini-backdrops, borders, and certificate borders. Different graphic shapes appear in different libraries. When you click on a square graphic placeholder, for example, the Graphics Browser that pops up will offer you these graphic shapes: square, column, row, and mini-backdrops. When you click on a border placeholder, the Graphics Browser that pops up will offer borders and certificate borders.

 To reach a Graphics Browser that offers all graphic shapes, select Object ➤ Add. The first item listed is Graphics. Click on this instead of one of the shapes offered and you go immediately to a Graphics Browser where you can search all shapes and all libraries. Selecting All Shapes and All Libraries as a search criterion is a quick way to search every graphic available at the same time.

Backdrop libraries are divided into backdrop shapes: tall and wide, with both options available on every Backdrops Browser.

All libraries have descriptive names designed to help you find the graphics you're looking for. For example, the Animals library contains—what else?—animal graphics. You can search graphic libraries or backdrop libraries by selecting a specific library by name or by selecting All Libraries and searching all libraries at once.

◆ Navigating the Graphics Browser

The task of sorting through more than 4,500 graphics to find just the right one would be insurmountable were it not for the Graphics Browser, shown in Figure 6.1. It makes short work of searching for a graphic by offering you a search strategy. Finding the right graphic for a project is as simple as making some basic decisions about your project and then searching the libraries for graphics that fit the search criteria.

In the Graphics Browser, you can search by graphic library or graphic shape, or you can do a more specific search by clicking on Search Options and selecting a search choice.

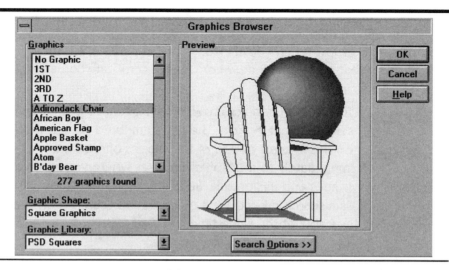

Figure 6.1: The Graphics Browser makes short work of searching for a graphic from the thousands available.

Starting a Project

First, what is the subject of your project? A birthday? A trip? A school dance? Once you've defined the subject, you can search for the right graphic by key words, either words that relate to the subject or theme or words that are a part of the text of the project.

Let's say your subject is a kids' burger party with dinosaurs as the theme. It might sound crazy to think you can find a graphic that fits this idea, but let's try.

Start a new project.

1. If you still have an open project, select File ➤ New ➤Stationery ➤ Postcard. If you're at the Select a Project dialog box, select Stationery ➤ Postcard.

2. At the orientation screen, hold down the Ctrl key and select Wide to go directly to the main project window.

In all the projects except Labels and Calendars, you can quickly reach the main project window from the Orientation screen by holding down the Ctrl key while clicking on the orientation of your project. This action bypasses the backdrop and layout options.

Broadening the Search Options

Now search for the perfect graphic, a burger-eating dinosaur:

1. Click on the New Object tool and select Add ➤ Square Graphic. A square graphic placeholder appears in the center of your blank page.

2. Double-click on the placeholder; the Graphics Browser pops up with Square Graphics selected under Graphic Shape. The default library is PSD Squares, with 277 available graphics.

 You can change the type of graphic in the Graphics Browser window. While you started with a square graphic in this search, you could switch to a column graphic, row graphic, or mini-backdrop by simply selecting one of these from the Graphic Shape drop-down list. The placeholder in the project will change its shape to accommodate the new graphic choice.

3. Click on the drop-down list arrow next to PSD Squares and you'll see all the libraries available for square graphics. You could search this list by library name for a burger-eating dinosaur, or you could broaden your search category by changing the Graphics Library choice to All Libraries. Because All Libraries will yield a lot more options, click on All Libraries. The graphics list now shows more than 3,000 square graphics available.

4. Narrow this list down by clicking on the Search Options button.

The Graphics Browser expands, as shown in Figure 6.2, to include some search options that enable you to specify narrower search criteria: Keywords, Category Keywords, Add Project Text, and Search Preferences.

Searching by Category

Let's begin with Category Keywords:

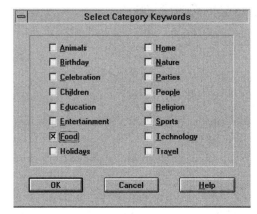

5. Click on the Category Keywords button, and up pops a list of 16 different keywords to aid in your search, as shown here. Because we're talking burgers, click on Food, then on OK to return to the Graphics Browser.

6. The word *Food* now appears in the Keywords box. Now click on Search; the Graphics Browser searches for square graphics with a food theme in all libraries.

The search finds 191 graphics that in some way include food; much fewer than 3,090, but still too many.

Searching by Multiple Keywords

Try narrowing the search further by adding *dinosaur* as a keyword.

7. In the Keywords box, type **dinosaur** next to *Food*. Include a space between the words but don't worry about upper- and lowercase—it doesn't matter to the search.

At this point you could click on Search and begin another search. However, just separating two keywords by a space activates the Match Any Keywords default, which would find graphics that relate either to

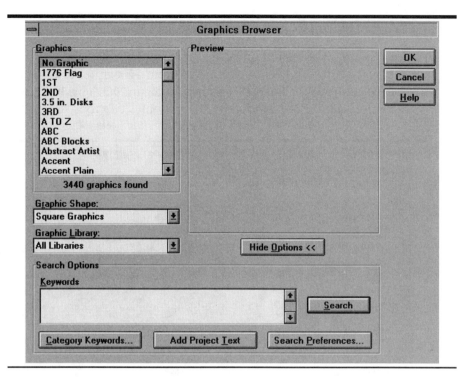

Figure 6.2: More options are displayed when you click on the Search
Options button.

food or to dinosaurs, but not necessarily both. If you began another
search now, the Browser would find 296 graphics; we would have added
more graphics by searching for food *or* dinosaurs.

8. Because you're looking for a graphic with dinosaurs *and* food, click
on Search Preferences. In the Search Preferences dialog box that

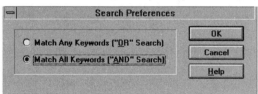

appears, select Match
All Keywords ("AND"
Search), as shown here,
to search for a graphic
that has both food and
a dinosaur. Click on OK.

9. Now search again. The graphic selection has dwindled to six
graphics (that's more like it).

10. Click through the choices in the graphics list; as you do so, check the preview window to see what they look like. They are all dinosaurs that are either eating, preparing to eat, or have eaten already. Amazingly enough, one of them—Brachiosaurus—is a dinosaur eating a burger, as shown in Figure 6.3. This is a great demonstration of how diverse the Graphics Library really is.

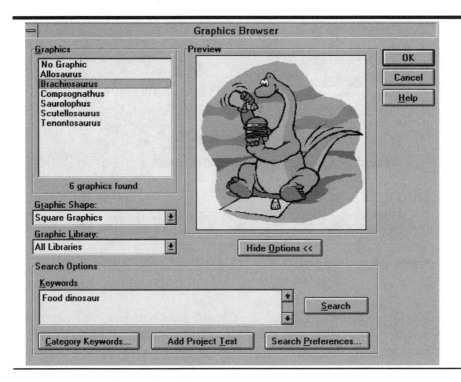

Figure 6.3: Searching on the keywords *food* and *dinosaur* finds six graphics, including this burger-eating dinosaur.

You could have found this dinosaur much faster by searching with the keywords *burger* and *dinosaur* from the very beginning. Let's try it.

1. Delete *Food* in the Keywords box and type **Burger**. Leave the word *Dinosaur*.

2. Click on Search Preferences and make sure Match All Keywords is still selected; you'll search for a graphic that matches both *burger* and *dinosaur*.

3. Now click on Search, and bingo! There's our burger-eating dinosaur, the Brachiosaurus. It is now the only graphic found in the search.

When a search is in progress, the Search button changes to a Stop button. If you want to stop the search, click on it.

Searching for an image is, as you've seen, easiest when you narrow your search by using specific keywords from the start. You can always broaden the search to less specific categories if you do not find a graphic right away.

Searching with Project Text

You can also search for a graphic by using any text you already have in the project, including text in word balloons, headlines, or text blocks. Let's try it.

1. Click on Cancel to return to the main project window. You still have a blank page except for the square graphic placeholder. Click on the New Object tool and select Text to add a text placeholder to the project.

2. Double-click on the text placeholder and, in the Edit Text dialog box that appears, type **HAVE A DINO BURGER**. Click on OK, and the text will be placed on your page.

3. Now double-click on the graphic placeholder to return to the Graphics Browser.

4. Select Search Options if they are not visible and click on Add Project Text. Text from the text box in your project now appears in the Keywords box: *HAVE DINO BURGER*. (Words like *a*, *an*, *and*, *the*, *from*, *to*, *by*, and *so* do not appear in the keywords box.) *HAVE* is not a word that will yield any results in search, so delete it from the keywords box. *DINO* may or may not help in the search. The program may know that *DINO* refers to a dinosaur, and it may not. Because we're not sure, leave it as a keyword.

5. Click on Search Preferences and select Match Any Keywords; the Browser will search for graphics that match either the word *BURGER* or the word *DINO*. Click on OK.

6. Under Graphics Library, select All Libraries, then click on Search. The search produces 11 graphics, one of them the burger-eating dinosaur and quite a few of them burgers.

 When you add project text, any keywords you already have in the keywords box will be replaced by the project text.

Searching for graphics is this easy. Define your search criteria and search either individual libraries or search all of them at once. We find that searching All Libraries at once is by far the best route.

Being able to browse the libraries for a suitable graphic is a great feature of Ensemble II. In the next section, you'll learn how to create a custom library that includes only the graphics you use most often; this consolidation will further shorten your search time.

◆ Merging Graphics Libraries

You can create a custom library by merging two or more libraries. Merging libraries gives you the opportunity to create libraries that cater to your particular Print Shop usage. When you merge libraries, you do not affect the original libraries; they remain intact. What you're really doing is merging copies of the libraries you've selected to create an entirely new library.

 You cannot modify the original Print Shop libraries. The program will not allow you to delete graphics from the original libraries, so don't worry about deleting graphics by mistake. However, once you've merged original libraries into a new custom library, you can delete, rename, or add to the copied graphics.

Preparing to Merge Libraries

Let's try our hand at merging libraries.

1. At the Select a Project dialog box, select Extras.

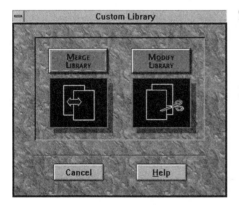

2. The Extra Features dialog box, shown in Figure 6.4, appears; choose Custom Libraries.

3. In the Custom Library dialog box, shown here, select Merge Library.

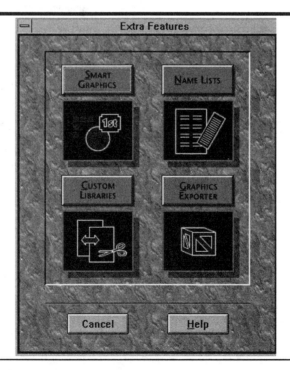

Figure 6.4: Clicking on Extras in the Select a Project dialog box brings up the Extra Features dialog box.

You'll see the Merge Libraries dialog box, shown in Figure 6.5. Because Square Graphics is selected in the Files of Type box, all square graphics libraries are listed. You can click on the Files of Type drop-down list arrow to access all Print Shop libraries, as follows:

Square Graphics (*.PSG—i.e., files ending in .psg)

Certificate Borders (*.CBR)

Borders (*.PBR)

Column Graphics (*.PCG)

Row Graphics (*.PRG)

Ruled Lines (*.PRL)

Seal Edges (*.PSE)

Seal Centers (*.PSI)

You can also search for other graphics libraries by changing your directory or drive on the left side of the Merge Libraries dialog box. However, any graphics you merge must be Print Shop graphics, meaning libraries with file names ending in .psg, .cbr, .pbr, .pcg, .prg, .prl, .pse, and .psi.

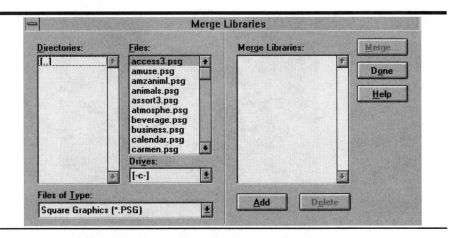

Figure 6.5:   The Merge Libraries dialog box presents you with options for merging libraries.

Keep in mind that these are libraries, not specific graphics. You cannot pick and choose graphics to merge into a library here. You must first merge libraries and then modify your new custom library by deleting or renaming graphics. See "Modifying Graphics Libraries" later in the chapter for more information.

Starting the Merge

Now for the actual library merge:

1. Select Square Graphics under Files of Type. The square graphics libraries appear in the Files area.

2. Select the libraries you want to merge; first choose the Animals library, named *animals.psg*. Highlight animals.psg and click on Add. The animals.psg library appears in the box labeled Merge Libraries.

 If you change your mind and do not want to merge the Animals library, click on Delete.

3. Now select another library (your turn to choose). Highlight it and click on Add.

4. To merge the libraries, click on the Merge button. The Name Graphic Library dialog box shown here pops up, with a default

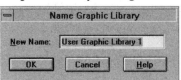

name of User Graphic Library 1 highlighted. This will be saved with the file name User1. (If this is not your first merge, the default name will be different.)

If you wanted to stick with the default name, you could just click on OK. But let's give the new library a different name. This name can be up to 8 characters long.

5. Type **Test1** and click on OK. The program will give the file an extension of .psg, and the merge is complete.

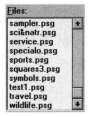

Scroll through the available files again; the new custom library called *test1.psg* will now be listed, as shown here. It's that simple.

You can further customize your new library by using the Modify Library option, as we'll discuss next.

6. Select Done to return to the Select a Project screen.

◆ Modifying Graphics Libraries

User-created custom libraries can be modified by deleting any unwanted graphics or by renaming graphics. As stated above, original Print Shop graphics libraries can only be modified if you first merge them into a custom library. They cannot be modified in their original form.

Preparing to Modify a Library

In order to modify a library, you need to use the Modify Library dialog box:

1. At the Select a Project dialog box, select Extras.

2. The Extra Features dialog box appears; choose Custom Libraries.

3. In the Custom Library dialog box, select Modify Library.

The Modify Library dialog box appears, as shown in Figure 6.6. While this dialog box lists all libraries, you will be able to modify only your custom libraries. As already noted above, you will not be able to modify original Print Shop libraries. If you try to modify an original library, a

prompt, shown here, will let you know that you cannot.

This dialog box also includes the option of selecting the graphic shape. If you have a lot of custom

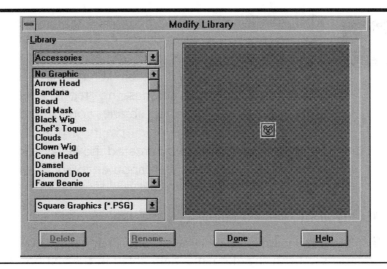

Figure 6.6:   The Modify Library dialog box offers you options for modifying a library, including deleting or renaming graphics.

libraries, this option might be helpful. For now, we have only one custom library, Test1, which we just made. This is the only library we can modify.

Modifying a Library

When you first enter the Modify Library dialog box, the default library selected is Accessories.

1. Click on the arrow next to Accessories and select Test1 from the drop-down list of libraries. All graphics stored in the library Test1 will be listed in the large center box.

2. Highlight any graphic in the list. It will appear in the preview window.

3. Click on Delete; the graphic will be deleted from the file.

When you delete a graphic, there is no prompt asking you if you're sure you want to delete it. Once you have hit the Delete key, the graphic is gone and you cannot undo the deletion. But because the custom library was created by merging two Print Shop libraries, the graphic still exists intact in one of the two Print Shop libraries you merged. Therefore, you could retrieve the graphic from its original file. If the deleted graphic is one you created, however, it's gone for good, unless you stored it in another library as well.

4. Highlight another graphic.

5. Click on Rename; the Rename Graphic dialog box, shown here, opens up with the old name highlighted in the text box. Give this

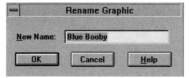

graphic a new name of up to 16 characters. (You can include spaces between words if you like.) Click on OK to give the graphic its new name.

Before we go on, let's do one more thing.

1. From the Library drop-down list, select Wildlife Squares. This is an original Print Shop Library. As noted above, you will not be able to modify this library. Let's see what happens if you try.

2. Highlight one of the graphics and click on Delete. A prompt pops up, warning you that you can delete only user-created libraries.

3. Click on Rename; the Rename Graphic dialog box pops up. You can type in a new name, but when you click on OK the same prompt appears, letting you know you cannot rename the graphic because it's an original Print Shop graphic.

That's all there is to it. With the Merge and Modify options, you can create a library that exactly fit your needs.

◆ **Endnotes**

You are now graphics library literate. You know how to:

- ◆ Recognize the file types in Print Shop libraries

- ◆ Browse for graphics and find a burger-eating dinosaur

- ◆ Set search options and use text in a project to find a graphic that creatively illustrates and enhances the text

- ◆ Create a custom library by merging two or more other libraries

- ◆ Modify a custom library

- ◆ Get a graphic back if by some chance you delete one you really want

You are a graphics library whiz—and now you're ready for Chapter 7, "Creating Special Graphics."

Creating Special Graphics

Your mission: to make some great special graphics

◆

The subject of this chapter is possibly the most exciting and creative part of PSD Ensemble II: creating your very own designs, adding that bit of pizzazz to your printed projects that you've been looking for. These are the design elements that will set your presentations in the realm of the most original ever seen by humankind.

OK, that statement may be a bit grandiose. What we're saying is that you can make some really great graphics with the special elements we'll cover in this chapter. All of this amazing creativity is reached through the most unassuming parts of this program, Smart Graphics and Seals.

◆ Customizing Smart Graphics

With Smart Graphics you can create special square graphics to use in your projects. There are three Smart Graphic styles available in PSD Ensemble II: initial caps, numbers, and timepieces. (Actually, there are four: the fourth is borders, but since borders are a totally different kind of graphic than the other three, we'll deal with them separately.)

Let's get started.

1. From the Select a Project screen, select Extras. The Extras menu pops up, offering Smart Graphics, Name List, Custom Libraries, and Graphics Exporter.

2. Select Smart Graphics: the Smart Graphics dialog box pops up (see Figure 7.1), offering four choices: Initial Caps, Numbers, Timepieces, and Borders.

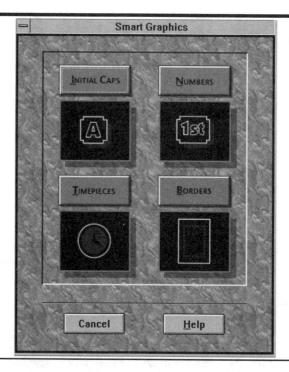

Figure 7.1:   The Smart Graphics dialog box offers four different graphics to create.

You can also reach smart graphics from the main project window by selecting Extras from the main menu, clicking on Smart Graphics, and choosing from the drop-down list offering Initial Caps, Numbers, Timepieces, and Borders. If you select Initial Caps, for instance, the Create an Initial Cap dialog box will pop up.

Designing an Initial Cap

The process of designing an initial cap takes place in the Create an Initial Cap dialog box, shown in Figure 7.2. This dialog box gives you a choice of upper- or lowercase letters in 3 text effects, 21 shapes, a range of Print Shop fonts (you may have more fonts available from other programs installed in your computer), 2 shadow effects, a choice of colors for text or text effects, and a variety of graphic backdrops. All of these elements enable you to create a unique initial cap which you can use to start a paragraph, embellish a letterhead, add style to a business card, customize a greeting card, or create your own personal monogram.

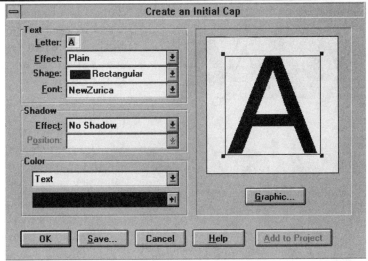

Figure 7.2: The Create an Initial Cap dialog box gives you a wide choice of fonts, styles, and colors, as well as a variety of graphic backdrops.

The design elements offered in the Create an Initial Cap dialog box are not limited to upper- and lowercase letters. You can type anything into the Letter box, including numbers or symbols. You can also design number graphics by choosing Smart Graphics ➤ Numbers, but special symbol graphics can only be designed in the Initial Cap area.

Let's go through the steps of designing an initial cap.

1. From the Smart Graphics dialog box, select Initial Cap to reach the Create an Initial Cap dialog box.

The default font is New Zurica, and the default letter is a capital *A*. Leave both of these as they are for this first creation. The Effect box in the Text area defaults to Plain, meaning that you have just a plain letter *A* without embellishment or modifications. Let's start to bring the letter *A* to life by seeing what our choices are and how they change the letter.

2. Click the arrow next to the Effect box. There are three options available to modify the letter's initial appearance. You can add a thin outline, a thick outline, or a highlight.

3. Click on each option to see how it changes the look of the letter *A*; the results are shown here. Note that the Highlight selection leaves a space between the letter and the outline.

4. When you're done looking, select Plain.

5. The next step is to change the shape of the letter. Click on the arrow next to the Shape box, and a drop-down list gives you 21 different shapes from which to choose. Go ahead and click on each choice so you can see how it changes the shape of the letter. All 21 options are shown here.

As you click through the options, you'll see that some distort the letter beyond recognition. Note how a change in shape can give the letter an added subtle meaning. Perspective Right, for instance, might say "movin' in," while Perspective Left could say "movin' on." Admittedly this example might be a little obscure, but this is the kind of reasoning used by many graphic designers in their design decisions. Let's face it: visual stimulation does motivate us to do a lot of things, even though it can be as subtle as the shape of a letter.

6. With the Effect option in the Shadow area, you can add a drop shadow or a silhouette to the letter, as shown here. If you choose

Drop Shadow, the Position box will let you place the shadow to the upper-right, upper-left, lower-right, or lower-left of the letter. Experiment with these choices to see how they look.

7. Next, you can change the color of the text, outline, or shadow. The Color box defaults to Text, but you can click on the arrow next to the box to access the other choices. Click on the colored box below to choose a new color for the element you want to change.

8. Finally, you can add a graphic backdrop. Click on the Graphic button, and the Graphics Browser pops up. The default library is Initial Caps, offering 35 graphics; however, you can select a graphic from any square graphic library, so you actually have over 3,000 graphics available.

To see how you can add meaning to a letter, try adding some specially designed initial caps to projects. We'll help get you started.

1. Cancel out of the Create an Initial Cap dialog box and select File ➤ New to access the Select a Project dialog box.

2. Select Certificates ➤ Ready Made ➤ Achievement. Then scroll through the list of ready-made projects and select Dancercise; it opens in the main project window.

3. Note the text box in the center. The text size here might be small enough to be unreadable, appearing only as a gray block. Click on this text box and the Edit Text dialog box pops up. The first word of the text is *Dancing*. Delete the letter *D* and click OK to return to the main project window.

4. Now save the certificate with the Save As command from the File menu. Name the new file *dancart*.

Your design challenge is to create an initial cap that will look like a dancing *D* to begin the word *dancing*.

5. Click on the Extras menu to start. Then select Smart Graphics ➤ Initial Caps and begin your design work.

6. For our example, choose a shape of Arc Up, with a gray drop shadow in the lower-right position and dark blue text with a light blue, thick outline in the New Zurica font.

7. When you have a design that you like, you'll want to see what it looks like on the certificate. Click on the Add to Project button.

8. You'll be prompted to save the initial cap as a graphic (you must do this before you can add it to the Dancercise Certificate). Click

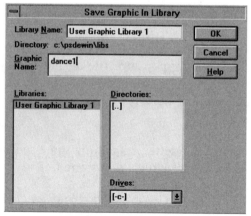

on OK; the Save Graphic In Library dialog box pops up, as shown here. Type **dance1** for the file name, since you might want to create a dance2, 3, 4, etc. until you get just the right design.

9. Note the Library Name box at the top of the Save Graphic In Library dialog box. Here you can select the library where the graphic will be stored. In this case, call the library *letter*.

10. Once you've given it a file name, the graphic will be saved and placed in the center of your project. Resize and move it around to the right position, as shown here.

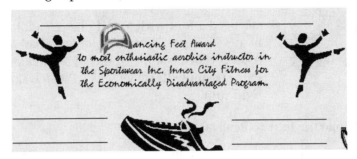

 If you save an initial cap without adding it to the project (by clicking on the Save button instead of the Add to Project button), you can retrieve it by adding a square graphic and double-clicking on its placeholder to reach the Graphics Browser. Change the library to your library name (in this case Letter), find the graphic (dance1), and insert it into the project.

Here's another idea. Let's create an original initial cap similar to those created by the scribes in ancient times, an initial cap designed to catch the reader's eye for a special piece of stationery.

1. Select Extras ➤ Smart Graphics ➤ Initial Caps to open the Create an Initial Cap dialog box.

2. Click on the Graphic button under the preview window. The 35 square graphics in the Initial Caps library are listed. Choose Pedestal to get started with the idea of creating a rather formal monogram for a notepad.

3. Click on OK and the Pedestal graphic becomes the backdrop for the letter *A*. Change the *A* to your initial. We changed ours to *C*.

4. Resize the letter until it sits on the pedestal. As you can see here, the New Zurica font does not work well with the Pedestal graphic.

We need a font with a serif or even additional elements to create the formal look we had in mind. After reviewing some of the styles included with PSD Ensemble II, we've selected Percival as just the right font.

5. Change the font to Percival.

6. Next, the letter needs to be more prominent. Choose the Silhouette option from Shadow Effect and separate the background from the letter with contrasting colors. The completed Initial Cap is shown here.

These are just a few examples of how simple it is to create your own initial cap, giving added pizzazz to a project. You can design numbers in Initial Caps as well, but the Numbers design area gives you the additional option of adding a suffix.

Designing a Number

Sometimes you want a number to stand out in your project. Let's say you want the world to know that you're number one in your business. You need to create a look that is instantly recognizable to your old clients as well as the new ones you would like to acquire.

1. Start by selecting File ➤ New, then select Stationery ➤ Ready Made ➤ Letterhead ➤ Graphics.

2. To design your special number graphic, click on Extras ➤ Smart Graphics ➤ Numbers.

The Create a Number dialog box pops up, as shown in Figure 7.3. The options offered here are the same as those offered in the Create an Initial Cap dialog box, except that you have the option of adding a suffix to your number, and when you click on the Graphic button, the default library is different.

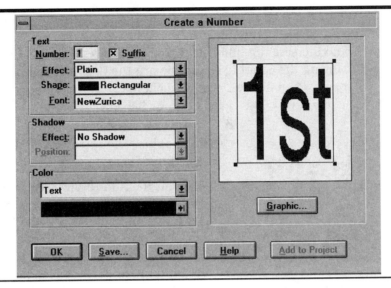

Figure 7.3: The Create a Number dialog box offers you 3 text effects, 21 text shapes, 65 fonts, 2 shadow effects, a choice of colors for text or text effects, and a variety of graphic backdrops.

3. The default number 1 has a suffix added to it so that it reads *1st*, not *1*. But "we're number first" doesn't make sense. To eliminate the suffix, uncheck the Suffix box next to the Number box. When this box is checked, it adds the suffixes *st*, *nd*, *rd*, and *th* to numbers as appropriate. Without the suffix, the number 1 is ready for you to begin your design work.

Here are some of the things that we did that you might want to try. We like the looks of the *1* in Tribune font with a shape of Perspective Right

and a drop shadow in the upper-right position, as shown here. Perspective Right opens the number slightly to invite the viewer in. The drop shadow reinforces this feeling, and its upper-right position makes the number stand out.

4. Make the appropriate adjustments so your number looks like ours, or choose your own look.

5. When you're done experimenting, click on the Graphic button; you're offered 21 graphics in the Decorative Numbers library. We could increase the number of graphic choices to over 3,000 by changing the Graphic Library box in the Graphics Browser to All Libraries. Out of the Decorative Numbers library choices, we like the one called Burst. Select it and click OK.

6. Resize the number and move it to fit over the graphic. The finished Number graphic is shown here.

7. Click on the Add to Project button, and you will be reminded that you must save it before you can add it to your letterhead. Save it as *one1* since you might decide to try another design or graphic selection. Save it to a library called Numbers. Just type Numbers as the name of the library in the Library Name box. Click OK and the number is added to the project.

8. As usual, your new number graphic appears in the center of the project. Move and resize it as necessary, then add text blocks for your business information and the "We're number" text preceding the 1.

Selecting a Timepiece

The Extras menu also gives you the opportunity to choose a timepiece to add to a project to make sure that the recipients of a meeting memo or party invitation know what time to show up.

1. To reach the Timepiece design area, select File ➤ New, and from the Select a Project dialog box, select Extras ➤ Smart Graphics ➤ Timepieces. (You can also reach the design area from the main project window by selecting the Extras ➤ Smart Graphics ➤ Timepieces.)

2. The Select a Timepiece dialog box, shown in Figure 7.4, appears. This dialog box offers 18 graphic timepiece designs. There are no other graphics available.

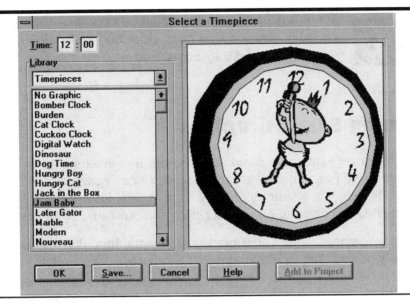

Figure 7.4:   The Select a Timepiece dialog box lets you choose from 18 custom timepieces.

You can select No Graphic in the Select a Timepiece dialog box, but it's not a real option. If you select No Graphic and click OK, you are sent back to the Smart Graphics menu or to the main project window, depending on which method you used to get here. Selecting No Graphic is the same thing as clicking on Cancel.

3. To create a timepiece, select one of the graphics and set the time in the box in the upper-left corner of the menu.

Some of the graphic designs in the Timepieces Library are analog and some are digital, as shown here.

There is no a.m. or p.m. indication on either analog or digital clocks. If you use a 24-hour clock and enter 19:00 as the time, it will be displayed as 7:00.

Naming Smart Graphics

All Smart Graphics are saved as square graphics in a user library before they are added to a project. You can name the library yourself; if you do not, it will be given a default user library name (User1, for example). Above, we created two libraries, one called Letters and one called Numbers.

Since Smart Graphics are stored as square graphics, they can be placed in any project. Your user library becomes another library offered when you browse for graphics. So among the list of available square graphics libraries, you should find one called Letters and one called Numbers.

It's a good idea to give your User Libraries descriptive names, as we did above. Descriptive names make it easier to find a specific graphic (which is a good reason to give the graphics themselves descriptive names as well), whether you're just browsing or using the Search options.

◆ Customizing Borders

Adding a custom border to a project can give your piece a distinctive look. To get into this part of PSD Ensemble II, from the main project

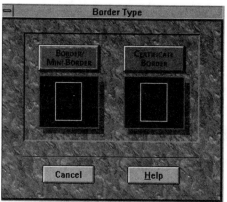

window select Extras ➤ Smart Graphics ➤ Borders. The Border Type dialog box appears. As shown here, your choices are Border/Mini-Border and Certificate Border.

The design process for both types of borders is basically the same. The only difference is that certificate borders are wider and have fewer arrangement choices.

Arranging a Border

Designing a border is a simple process of arranging square graphics into a design that suits your creative vision. You can choose from the 3,000 square graphics in the PSD program, which you can arrange in a variety of ways.

You choose the arrangement in the Border Arrangement area of the Create a Border dialog box, shown in Figure 7.5. A sample illustration of the border appears in the preview area to the right. Figure 7.5 illustrates the Single Piece Repeating arrangement. The other three arrangement options—Corners and Rails, Alternating Rails, and Rails with Centerpieces—are shown in Figures 7.6 through 7.8.

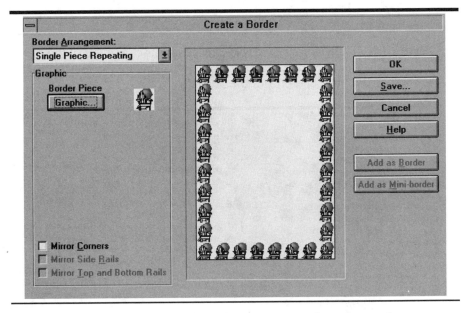

Figure 7.5: The Single Piece Repeating arrangement is made up of one square graphic which repeats over and over around the border.

To change the arrangement, just click on the arrow next to the Border Arrangement box and select the arrangement you want. The Graphic area just below will change to reflect the different graphic elements that make up the new arrangement. Click on the Graphic button below each element to choose a graphic for that element.

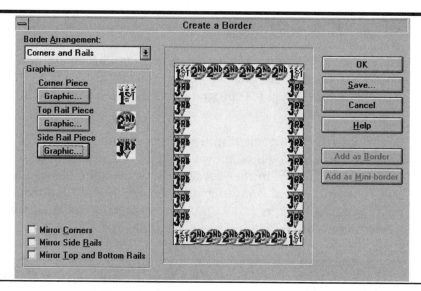

Figure 7.6: The Corners and Rails arrangement is composed of three different graphics, one for the corners, one for the top and bottom rails, and one for the side rails.

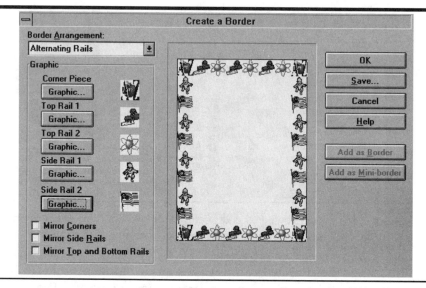

Figure 7.7: The Alternating Rails arrangement is composed of five different graphics: one for the corners, two (alternating) for the top and bottom rails, and two (alternating) for the side rails. This arrangement is not available for certificate borders.

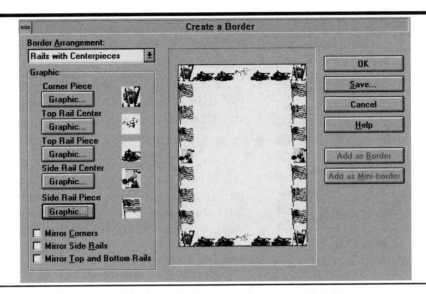

Figure 7.8: The Rails with Centerpieces arrangement is made up of five different graphics: one for the corners, one for the top and bottom rails, one for the center of the top and bottom rails, one for the side rails, and one for the center of the side rails. This arrangement is not available for certificate borders.

The Create a Border dialog box also offers three mirroring options. You can mirror corners, side rails, or top and bottom rails by clicking on the appropriate check boxes in the lower-left corner of the dialog box. We'll take a look at some mirror images in the next part of this chapter.

Choosing Border Graphics

Now that we know about border arrangements, let's try creating a few borders.

1. Select Extras ➤ Smart Graphics ➤ Borders ➤ Border/Mini-Border; the Create a Border dialog box pops up. The default arrangement is Single Piece Repeating, and the preview shows a solid black border.

2. Click on the Graphic button under Border Piece in the Graphic area. You'll see a selection of 277 square graphics in the PSD Squares library. Choose Frog and look at it in the preview area. Note that the frog is facing left.

3. Click OK and you return to the Create a Border dialog box with the frog repeated as a border in the preview window. All of the frogs are facing left.

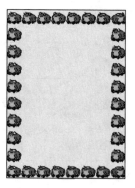

4. Click on the Mirror Corners check box. The two right corners become mirror images of the left corners, as shown here.

5. Now change the border arrangement to Corners and Rails. When the program asks you if you want to save the frog border, click on No. All of the frogs disappear and you have three graphic elements to fill: Corner Piece, Top Rail Piece, and Side Rail Piece.

6. Click on the Graphic button below Corner Piece, choose American Flag, and click on OK. A flag appears in each corner of the preview window, with the flagpole on the left side.

7. Click on the Graphic button for the top rail piece and choose Cherry Pie. Click on OK. A row of cherry pie slices appears across the top and bottom row of the sample page.

8. Click on the Graphic button under Side Rail Piece. You've probably figured out by now that we're making a border that's as American as cherry pie. (Okay, in the saying it's apple pie, but who's checking? We like the way the cherry pie looks.) So what else do we need? Mom, of course. There's an appropriate graphic in this library called Woman Icon. Click on it, then click on OK; the side rails in the preview fill with Mom's left profile.

9. Check the Mirror Side Rails box; Mom's profile changes from left to right on the right side of the page. Check the Mirror Top and Bottom Rail box; the pies turn upside-down on the bottom row. Check Mirror Corners, and the flagpoles move to the right on the right side of the page. The result looks like Figure 7.9.

As you can see, the graphics can be used in different combinations creating variations almost without limit.

Figure 7.9: Checking all the mirroring options produces some interesting and some unacceptable results.

Saving a Custom Border

As with the other Smart Graphics selections, you must save borders before they can be used in your project. The process for saving a border is exactly like saving a initial cap, number, or timepiece, as discussed above.

You have the option in the Create a Border dialog box to add your border creation to the project as either a border or a mini-border. If you save your creation as a border, it will become a permanent border on the project. Like a PSD original border, you will not be able to resize or move it. You will be able to lighten it in the main project window using the Shading Selector on the toolbar. On the other hand, if you save your creation as a mini-border, it will act just like an original Print Shop mini-border, meaning you will be able to resize and move it in a project.

Custom borders are stored in a user library named by you, just as you named the Letters and Numbers libraries. The Search option in the Borders Browser includes user-created borders. Be sure to give your borders descriptive names so you can find them again easily.

Adding a Custom Border to a Project

To automatically add a custom border to the main project window, click on the Add as Border or Add as Mini-border button in the Create a Border dialog box. After you give your creation a name, it will be added.

If you click on OK instead of Add as Border or Add as Mini-border, the custom border will not be added to the project. It will instead be saved to the library and file you designate.

To add a saved custom border later, go to the main project window, select Object ➤ Add ➤ Border or Mini-border. The Graphics Browser pops up. Select your library from the Graphic Library list, select the border name from the list of graphics, and click OK. The border is added to the project.

◆ Designing a Seal

Official-looking seals can give letterhead, envelopes, or almost any piece of printed material a distinctive look. With PSD Ensemble II, you can create seals of your own for any project. You can also use the Seal feature to design a creative logo for your business or activity.

Seals are circular and can include a center graphic, an edge graphic, and basic text. You can choose any or all of these design options when you create your seal. Seals are always designed from the main project window, either by adding a seal placeholder or by clicking on a seal placeholder that is already part of a certificate layout. Let's look at adding a seal placeholder and creating a seal.

1. To start, select Object ➤ Add ➤ Seal.

2. A seal placeholder appears in the center of your project. Click on this placeholder to open the Seal dialog box.

Adding a Graphic

The Seal dialog box, shown in Figure 7.10, includes two graphic options, Center and Edge. You can choose graphics from either one of these or both.

3. Click on Center; the Select a Seal Center dialog box, shown in Figure 7.11, offers 53 different graphics. As usual, you can click through the graphics and see them previewed. When you've made your selection, click on OK to return to the Seal dialog box with the center graphic in place.

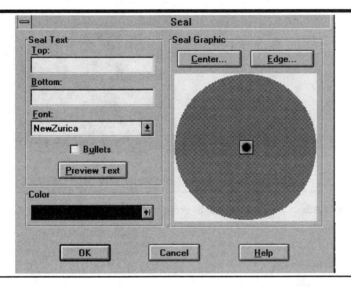

Figure 7.10:   Seals are designed in the Seal dialog box, which appears when you click on an existing seal or a seal placeholder.

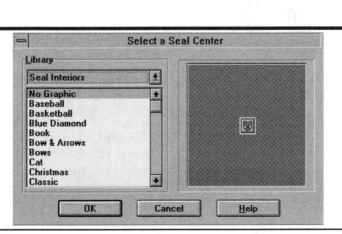

Figure 7.11:   The Select a Seal Center dialog box offers 53 interior graphics.

4. Click on Edge; the Select a Seal Edge dialog box, shown in Figure 7.12, offers 23 different circle designs for the outside edge of the seal. When you've made your selection, click on OK to return to the Seal dialog box with the edge graphic in place.

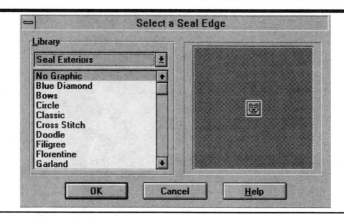

Figure 7.12:   The Select a Seal Edge dialog box offers 23 exterior designs.

Many of the edge graphics coordinate with center graphics. Coordinated graphics have the same name. For example, Blue Diamond in the Select a Seal Edge dialog box is the coordinating element for Blue Diamond in the Select a Seal Center dialog box. Both are shown here. Other coordinated centers and edges include Florentine, Lace, Link, Oak, Wood Rose, Primary, and Roses.

Adding Text

Text can be composed in any available font and placed in the upper and lower halves of the seal. Top seal text curves above the center graphic. Bottom seal text curves below the center graphic.

5. To enter top text, simply place the cursor in the text box marked Top and begin typing. Do the same in the box marked Bottom for the bottom text. Both top and bottom text can be up to 63 characters long. Seal text is designed to fit into a small area; thus it is small in size and not very readable. Whatever you place here should be succinct.

6. Click on the arrow next to the font box to change the font as you please. Text size cannot be changed.

7. Place a check in the Bullets box. When you select this box, bullets will be placed on each side of the seal between the top and bottom text.

8. Click on the Preview Text button to see all the elements in place in the preview window. The seal previewed here has all the available

elements: center graphic, edge graphic, text, and bullets.

You can change the color of monochrome graphics, bullets, and text using the Color area of the Seal dialog box. Whatever color you choose becomes the color for all elements (you cannot color text one color and monochrome graphics another color). If the graphics are already in color, the color you select will apply only to the text and bullets.

 You can change the color of monochrome graphics, text, and bullets in the main project window also: select the seal, click on the Item Selector, and choose Object, then use the Color Selector to change the color. To change the color behind the seal, select Behind Object from the Item Selector and then select a color.

Saving a Customized Seal

Unlike smart graphics, seals are not saved to a library. They are saved only as a part of a project. However, you can save one as a graphic file if you like. Here's how.

1. Open a new project (a sign or letterhead would be good).

2. Select Start From Scratch and then choose either a wide or tall orientation. When you select the orientation, hold down the Ctrl key and you will bypass the backdrop and layout options to go directly to the main project window with a blank page.

3. On this blank page, create a seal using the techniques mentioned above.

4. Once you have created the seal, resize it to fit the full page or as close to full as you can get.

5. Select File ➤ Save As and save the project as a TIFF file in an appropriate library (for instance, one called Seals).

Now you can import this TIFF file into any project and resize and move it to the area you want it to cover. You can use this technique to create a logo and import it into letterhead, business cards, labels, or whatever you like.

◆ Endnotes

Now you know how to create your own custom graphics. You can:

◆ Design an initial cap and add a graphic to give it style and mood

◆ Create a dramatic number graphic to punctuate an occasion or make a point

◆ Make a timepiece that's set for the exact time you want all your friends to show up for an event

◆ Make a special border with alternating or mirroring graphics, and search from over 3,000 graphics available for the design

◆ Create a seal with coordinating graphics and add color to the design

◆ Design a logo and save it for other projects

You are a special graphics whiz. You're ready for Chapter 8, "Importing Images."

Importing Images

Your mission: to import a graphic and a photo

◆

Importing a graphic or photo into a Print Shop project is easy, provided the graphic's file format is compatible with Print Shop. The import function supports a variety of graphic file formats (graphic types), and it supports a high-resolution file format for importing photos.

◆ Importing Graphics

Four types of graphics can be imported into a Print Shop project:

Windows Bitmaps	BMP
Windows Metafiles	WMF
Tagged Image Files	TIFF
Encapsulated Postscript Files	EPS

 Different programs save graphics as different file types. A graphic from Microsoft Word's Clipart directory, for example, is saved as a Windows Metafile (WMF), while a graphic from Broderbund's Kid Pix for Windows is a bitmap file (BMP).

To import an image, whether it's a BMP, WMF, TIFF, or EPS file:

1. Either click on Object ➤ Add or click on the New Object tool.
2. Select Import.
3. Find the graphic you want to add.
4. Click on OK to import it.

It's that simple. Give it a try with this new project:

1. Select File ➤ New ➤ Signs & Posters ➤ Start From Scratch ➤ Wide ➤ Blank Page ➤ No Layout.

You'll find yourself at the main project window, ready to begin importing.

Choosing a Graphic Format

To import a graphic:

2. Pull down the Object menu and select Add. You will be offered a list of objects you can add to your project: Graphic, Square Graphic, Row Graphic, Column Graphic, and so on. You will find Import at the very bottom of the list.

3. Click on Import. The Import Graphic dialog box pops up, as shown in Figure 8.1.

Some BMP files are listed here and the drive and directory are c:\deskscan. We happen to have several BMP files at this location, and the program automatically starts looking for BMP files. In our case, it found the ones shown in Figure 8.1. That does not mean that these are the only BMP files, just the first ones found by the program. Your Import Graphic dialog box may or may not have any BMP files listed when it first comes up.

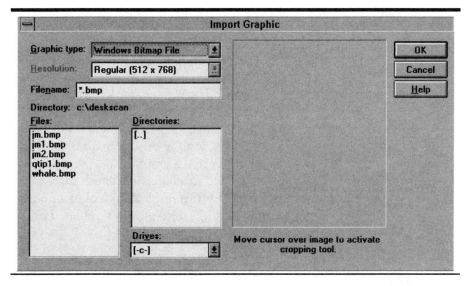

Figure 8.1: The Import Graphic dialog box allows you to import graphics saved in different file formats.

4. Select a graphic type from the list: BMP, WMF, TIFF, or EPS. The default is BMP.

Which graphic type you choose will be dictated by the graphic you want to import. If it's stored on a disk or in another program as a TIFF, you'll select TIFF as you file format, for example. On the other hand, if you're importing a graphic stored in the Clipart directory in Microsoft Word, the file format would be WMF, since all these graphics files are stored as Windows Metafiles.

5. If you have Microsoft Word, select Windows Metafile as your file type. The directory should automatically change to your Word directory. If it does not, type in the Clipart location. All the files stored as WMF graphics will be listed in the Files box. Click on one and it will be previewed.

Looking at Available Files

You can navigate through your drives and directories by typing the directory path or by clicking through the drive and directory lists. You could, for example, insert a disk containing a special graphics library and search it for a graphic to import by clicking on the letter for the floppy drive (usually A or B) in the Drives box, then choosing the file type, and then selecting available graphics to see them in preview.

If you browse through your system, you'll find graphics in compatible file formats in various programs. As previously mentioned, there are Microsoft Word Clipart and Kid Pix BMPs, among others. In addition, any BMP, TIFF, WMF, and EPS graphic files you have created in or imported from another source can be accessed and imported into Print Shop. For example, we scanned in a photograph, shown here, and saved it as a TIFF in our deskscan directory.

BMP files can be cropped before they are imported into the project. Cropping is available only for BMP files, not for WMF, TIFF, or EPS files. Refer to the "Cropping Photos" section later in this chapter for more on using this cropping option.

Importing a Graphic

Once you've selected a file (and cropped it to your liking if it's a BMP), all you have to do is click OK to import it into a project. The graphic will be placed in the center of the project window. You can then move and resize the graphic as desired. Print Shop graphics are scalable graphics, meaning they can be resized without losing shape or clarity. Imported files, on the other hand, may be scaled bitmap files, meaning they are not designed to be resized or reshaped. Scaled bitmap files will not appear smooth if you resize them. If you enlarge an imported scaled bitmap file, the image will begin to break up, or *pixelize*. For this reason, imported graphics are best used in their imported size.

 Imported color graphics will always display in color if you have a color monitor. Even if you are working in grayscale, imported color graphics will be displayed in color. Changing the color preference in the main project window does not affect the way imported color graphics are displayed.

An Importing Tip

A Print Shop project can be saved as a Windows Metafile (WMF), TIFF Bitmap file (TIFF), or Windows Bitmap file (BMP). When you save the project, just select TIFF, for example, as your file type rather than the standard Print Shop extension. If you were saving a sign, the standard extension would be .pds (Print Shop sign). Change this to .tif and save.

Now you have a TIFF file which can be imported into another Print Shop project. So you could, for example, start a second sign project and import the first sign project as a graphic, creating an entirely different look and style, as shown in Figure 8.2. Also, saved as a WMF, TIFF, or BMP, the project can be inserted into a compatible program outside Print Shop, such as Microsoft Word.

◆ Importing Photos

You can import photos from a CD-ROM drive or from BMP or TIFF images. Print Shop gives you a selection of 20 photos to import into your projects. These photos are stored in the ClipPix file on the Print Shop CD; they are not loaded into your system when Print Shop is loaded.

Figure 8.2:   You can save a project as a TIFF file, then import it as a graphic into another project.

The photos in the ClipPix file can be used fairly liberally in your projects. With a few restrictions, they can be copied, modified and incorporated in materials for personal use, in advertising and promotional materials, and as part of a product for sale. Consult the booklet inserted into the CD-ROM container for specifics.

To look at the Print Shop photos:

1. Insert the PSD Ensemble II CD into your CD-ROM drive.

2. Select Object ➤ Add ➤ Import. The Import Graphic dialog box pops up.

3. From the Graphic type drop-down list, select Photo CD File. The program should automatically access the CD and list the available photos in the Files box. If it does not automatically access your CD, change the drive to your CD drive. As usual, you can highlight the files to preview them.

4. Click on the photo named *farmland.pcd*. A pasture scene with grazing horses and part of a red-roofed barn is previewed, as shown in Figure 8.3.

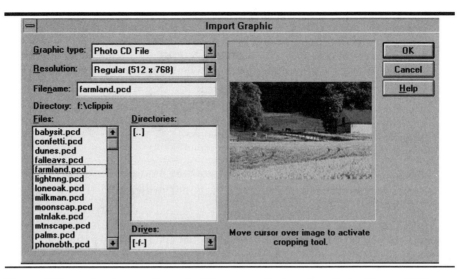

Figure 8.3:   The Import Graphic dialog box displays the photo files available, previewing the highlighted photo.

In the Import Graphic dialog box you can also choose a resolution for your imported photo. Photo CD images can be imported in one of five different resolutions:

Extra Low	128 × 192 dots per inch
Low	256 × 384 dots per inch
Regular	512 × 768 dots per inch
High	1,024 × 1,536 dots per inch
Extra High	2,048 × 3,072 dots per inch

The more dots per inch, the smoother the image will appear and the less likely it will pixelize if you choose to enlarge it. However, higher-resolution images also take more memory to display, print, and save. The memory requirements for each resolution choice are as follows:

Extra Low	2.5MB
Low	3MB
Regular	7.5MB
High	15MB
Extra High	30MB

These memory requirements decrease in proportion to how much of the photo you use (we discuss cropping photos next). If you use only a small part of the total image, the memory requirements are considerably less; in this case, it might make sense to use the highest resolution so you can resize as needed and still have a great-looking picture.

Cropping Photos

As with BMP files, photos can be cropped before you import them. As you highlight the available photos, you'll notice that the following text appears under the preview box:

Move cursor over image to activate cropping tool.

This means exactly what you think it means. You can crop the photo, choosing to import into your project only that portion of the picture you want. To crop and import a photo:

1. The farmland.pcd photo should already be selected. If it's not, click on it. We'll be cropping out the grazing white horses in the left side of the photo.

2. Move your cursor over the picture. The cursor arrow changes to crosshairs. Position the crosshairs at the upper-left corner above the horses.

3. Hold down your left mouse button and drag over the horses, drawing a box around them, as shown here. When you're finished, release your mouse button. If you are not satisfied, just click anywhere on the screen and the box will disappear. Then draw it again.

4. When it's just right, click on OK. The cropped image will be imported into the center of the main project window, as shown here. You can then resize and move the image.

Resizing Photos

Photos in the main project window can be resized or moved to match your creative vision for the project. Be aware that photos will pixelize as you enlarge them; while this may be OK if it's an effect you're aiming for, it won't be OK if you don't want the effect.

Photos in the project window behave the same as Print Shop graphics. To resize a photo keeping the same aspect ratio, select it, then drag one of its handles. To resize the image without maintaining the aspect ratio, hold down the Ctrl key while you drag a handle.

◆ Endnotes

While the graphics offered by the Print Shop program are considerable, you are not restricted to these. You can import more graphics from other programs or from a disk or CD and you can do it quite easily. You know how to:

◆ Choose a graphic type to import

◆ Find a graphic by searching drives and directories

◆ Store a Print Shop project as a BMP, WMF, or TIFF file and then import it into another project or program

◆ Access photos from the ClipPix images on the Print Shop CD

◆ Select a resolution for a photo import

◆ Crop a BMP graphic and a photo

◆ Move and resize an imported image

You're ready for Chapter 9, "Exporting Graphics."

Exporting Graphics

Your mission: to export graphics and graphics libraries for use outside of Print Shop

◆

The Graphics Exporter in PSD Ensemble II is a handy tool for exporting Print Shop graphics so that they can be used in other graphics or desktop publishing programs. This export option gives you access to Print Shop graphics in any program you choose. In addition to exporting to a file, you can also export to the printer, printing all or a portion of a library.

Exporting a graphic using the Graphics Exporter is so quick and easy that it's hard to believe you're actually doing it. You can export one graphic or a series of graphics—even a whole library—with a single export command.

Simply choose the graphic or graphics you want, select a destination file or printer, and you're ready to export.

You can export graphics from any of Print Shop's graphic libraries as well as any user libraries you create. The Graphics Exporter even allows you to preview a graphic before you export it to make sure it's the one you want.

◆ Opening the Graphics Exporter

The Graphics Exporter is easily accessed, whether or not you've opened Print Shop. You can enter the Graphics Exporter in three different ways:

Ensemble
Graphics
Exporter

◆ Before opening Print Shop, click on the Ensemble Graphics Exporter icon, shown here.

◆ Inside Print Shop, choose Extras from the Select a Project dialog box, and the Extra Features dialog box will appear. Click on Graphics Exporter.

◆ From Print Shop's main project window, open the Extras menu and choose Export Graphics.

After you have selected the Graphics Exporter using one of these three methods, the Print Shop Deluxe Graphics Exporter dialog box, shown in Figure 9.1, appears on your screen.

◆ Choosing a Graphic

You can select one graphic to export, or you can select a series of graphics and export all of them with one command. To select a single graphic to export:

1. Open the Graphics Exporter dialog box using one of the methods listed above.

2. In the Graphics Exporter dialog box, click on the Graphic Library drop-down list to view the names of all Print Shop libraries and any user libraries.

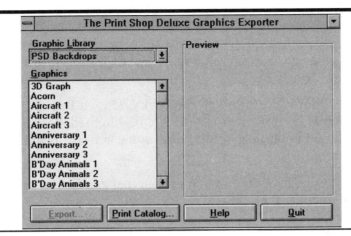

Figure 9.1: Whichever method you use to open the Graphics Exporter, this dialog box will appear on your screen.

3. Click on a library to view the names of all the graphics in that library, or select All Libraries to see the names of all available graphics. For this example, select PSD Squares.

 If you need some help finding the right graphic for a particular project, use the advanced Search options in the Graphics Browser to pinpoint the graphic(s) you want. You'll need to do this before you select the Graphics Exporter. The Graphics Browser is discussed in more detail in Chapter 1.

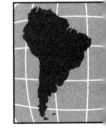

4. Once you find the graphic you'd like to export, click on it to highlight it. For this example, choose B'day Bear. The graphic appears in the preview area, as shown here, and is now ready for export.

Let's say you want to export all of the graphics listed between B'day Bear and Beach Ball in the PSD Squares library. It would be tedious to select and export them one at a time. But you can use the Shift key to select a block of graphics to export or the Ctrl key to pick and choose graphics to export. Let's give this a try.

1. Click on the first graphic you want to select—in this case, B'day Bear.

2. Hold down the Shift key and click on Beach Ball. All the graphics from B'day Bear to Beach Ball are highlighted. Because you have selected multiple graphics, no graphic appears in the preview window.

If you chose to click OK now, all the selected graphics would be exported as a group under their Print Shop file names to whatever destination you designated.

3. Release the Shift key and click on Beach Ball again. Now only Beach Ball is selected and it appears in the preview window.

4. With Beach Ball already selected, hold down the Ctrl key and click on B'day Bear again. Only Beach Ball and B'day Bear are highlighted, and once again no graphic appears in the preview window.

If you chose to click OK now, you would export only Beach Ball and B'day Bear together under their Print Shop file names to whatever destination you chose.

◆ Exporting a Graphic

Before you export a graphic, make sure you know what file format the graphic needs to be in so it is compatible with its destination.

Designating a File Type

You can export a graphic as one of the following file types:

BMP	Windows Bitmap
TIFF	Tagged Image File
WMF	Windows Metafile
EPS	Encapsulated PostScript

The Graphics Exporter's EPS format saves EPS files without preview. This means that when you import these EPS files into a project outside Print Shop, you will not see a preview of the graphic. Rather, you see only a box representing the graphic's location. You can resize and move this box but you will not see the actual graphic until you print the project. Also, keep in mind that it takes a PostScript printer to print an EPS file. If you don't have a PostScript printer, do not export graphics as EPS files.

To assign your graphic a name and file format:

1. Highlight Beach Ball and click on Export. A dialog box named *Export 'Beach Ball' as* appears, in which you can name your file,

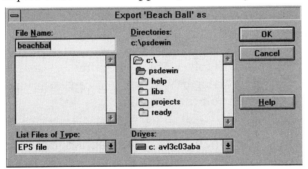

choose a file format, and select a destination, as shown here. When you export multiple graphics, this dialog box will simply be titled *Export Graphics as*.

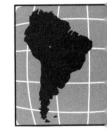

2. In the File Name box, the default name is *beachbal* (the first eight letters of the graphic's name in the library list). Type **beach1** as the graphic's new name.

3. Click on the List Files of Type drop-down list and select Windows Bitmap as the file format for the graphic.

If you have selected multiple graphics for export, you cannot change any of their names. They will all be exported under the names given to them in Print Shop. You can change their names in Windows File Manager or Windows Explorer outside Print Shop after they have been exported, if you like.

Choosing a Destination

You're almost ready to export the beach ball graphic. But first, plan a destination for your Print Shop graphics. It's a good idea to create a special directory on your hard drive or designate a floppy disk for your graphics files so you can access the exported graphics easily. You might even want to create individual directories for the different file formats.

For example, if you elect to store exported graphics on your main drive, you could create a directory called \psdewin\exports with subdirectories labeled tiff, bmp, wmf, and eps.

Now choose a destination for your graphic:

1. Select a folder to export your graphic file into. For this example, keep the default destination, \psdewin.

2. Click on OK and it's done.

You have now exported the Beach Ball graphic to a file called beach1.bmp in the \psdewin folder. You are returned to the Print Shop Deluxe Graphics Exporter dialog box, where you can export additional graphics, print libraries, or quit the program.

 Remember that when you export graphics, only copies of the original files are exported. The Print Shop files remain intact and the original libraries are not altered in any way.

◆ Exporting a Library

With PSD Ensemble II, you have the option of exporting an entire library or a page of a library by using the Print Catalog option in the Graphics Exporter dialog box. You can export a library or library page to a file outside of Print Shop or to a printer.

You can print catalogs in color or black and white, depending on the type of printer you have. Complete libraries exported to a file will always be exported in the color of the original Print Shop file—in other words, color graphics will be exported in color, and black and white graphics will be exported in black and white.

When you print exported graphic libraries, 12 to 21 graphics will fit on one page, depending on the graphics' size.

Printing a Catalog

You can select which pages of a library you want to export. For example, you can export only pages 1 and 2 of a library to the printer. However, it is difficult to decide which pages of a library to print, since you don't know which page specific graphics will print on.

To print a page from the PSD Squares catalog:

1. In the Graphics Export dialog box, make sure PSD Squares is the current library. If it's not, click on the Graphic Library pull-down list and select PSD Squares.

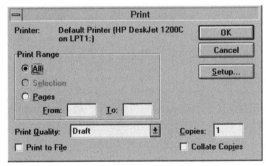

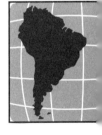

2. Click on Print Catalog; the Print dialog box, shown here, pops up.

3. The default setting for Print Range is All, but for this example we only want to print one page. Click on Pages and type 1 in the From box and 1 in the To box.

4. Because this is a test, you may want to change the Print Quality box from the default setting (High) to Low.

5. Type the number of copies you'd like to print in the Copies box, in this case **1**.

6. Click on OK to print page 1 of the PSD Squares catalog.

As you've just discovered, PSD Squares prints 12 graphics per page. You can now calculate which pages to select in order to print a particular series of graphics from this library. For example, if you want to print graphics 20 through 26 from the PSD Squares library, you'd print pages 2 and 3. (Graphics 20 through 24 will print on page 2 and graphics 25 and 26 will print on page 3). Other libraries may print a different number of graphics per page, so it's a good idea to print a sample page as we just did before you do your calculations.

You can only use the Graphics Exporter to print libraries or pages of libraries. To print a single graphic, open a project window, import the graphic, and then print it from there. See Chapter 8 for information about importing graphics.

If you are printing more than one copy of a library, you may want to collate the printed pages. To do this, check the Collate Copies box in the lower-right corner of the Print dialog box; the computer will print all of the pages of one copy before printing the next copy. If Collate Copies is not selected, the printer will print all of the copies of page one, followed by all copies of page two, and so on, and you will have to sort them manually.

Printing to File

The Print dialog box also offers a Print to File option, which lets you copy an entire library to a disk. This is particularly useful if you do not have a color printer and want to print a graphic library (called a *catalog* here) in color. You can copy the graphic library to a disk, take the disk to a computer that has a color printer, and print.

When you check the Print to File box, a prompt pops up, asking you to designate where you want the file saved. Type in the specific location, including drive, directory and file name.

When you're printing to a file, you'll see a box that says the catalog is printing on your printer. Actually, it's printing to the disk, not the printer. Print Shop has no prompt that says that it's printing to a file, so it defaults to the one that says it's printing to a printer.

Exiting the Graphics Exporter

When you're all done exporting, just click on the Quit button in the
Print Shop Deluxe Graphics Exporter dialog box to exit the program.

◆ Endnotes

You're ready to export graphics from Print Shop on your own. You can:

◆ Open the Graphics Exporter

◆ Locate and preview the graphics you want to export

◆ Choose a destination for your graphics

◆ Export graphics to a printer or to a file

◆ Print pages of graphics from a library—or the whole library itself

Now on to some finishing touches in Part III.

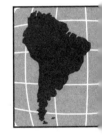

Part Three:

Finishing Touches

Working with Text and Headlines

Your mission: to master all the ways to add text to a project

◆

Text can be added to a project in six different formats:

- ◆ Text blocks
- ◆ Headlines
- ◆ Title blocks
- ◆ Signature blocks
- ◆ Word balloons
- ◆ Quotes and verses

We have already touched on some of these in other chapters, but in this chapter we'll cover them more completely and introduce you to the text formats we have not yet explored, such as word balloons and quotes and verses. Examples of these text formats are shown in Figure 10.1. Quotes and verses is not included because it does not have its own text box, but rather is added to a text block or a word balloon using a special button.

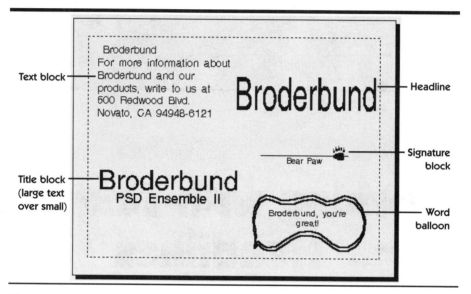

Figure 10.1: Text can be added to a project in several different formats.

◆ Editing Text Blocks

The Edit Text dialog box, shown in Figure 10.2, pops up when you double-click on a text block or when you select a text block and then select Object ➤ Edit. In this dialog box, you can add text (your own or quotes and verses); select a font and its size, style, and color; justify text; and merge lists. Once you have made your selections, you can preview all the text with its selected attributes before you add it to the project.

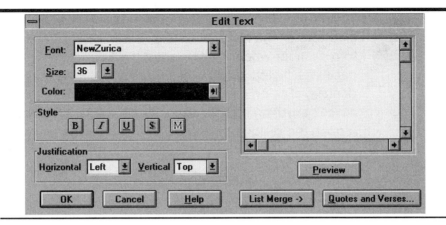

Figure 10.2: Double-clicking on a text block opens the Edit Text dialog box.

Choosing Text Attributes

Changing the text characteristics of your projects is accomplished by changing font, size, color, style, and justification. It's the individual attributes that make up the total look of the presentation, or as it's sometimes referred to, its *style*. Making changes to the text after your project is underway is easy with PSD Ensemble II. Let's start a project so you can see exactly what you can do with a text block.

1. If you have an open project, select File ➤ New ➤ Signs & Posters ➤ Ready Made ➤ Business ➤ Recycling Fundraiser, or from the Select a Project dialog box select Signs & Posters ➤ Ready Made ➤ Business ➤ Recycling Fundraiser.

There are two different text blocks on this sign. One begins *Bring your old…* and the second begins *Make Earth….* Let's work with the first text block.

2. Double-click on *Bring your old…* to open the Edit Text dialog box.

All of the text in the text box is highlighted. When text is highlighted like this, any change that you make to the text attributes will change all of the highlighted text. If you want to change attributes for only a part of the text, highlight just that text.

When text is highlighted, any numeric or alphabetic key you hit erases all the highlighted text. This is especially important to remember when you first enter the Edit Text dialog box because all existing text is highlighted. If you erase text accidentally, click on Cancel to exit the Edit Text dialog box. This cancels anything you did and restores the text. You can then reopen the dialog box and begin editing again.

For now, let's leave all the text highlighted and change its attributes.

3. The current font on this project is Moderne. Click on the Preview button to see what it looks like. To see other available fonts, click on the arrow next to the Font box. As you highlight each font, it will be previewed (as long as you're still in the preview mode). Select Cornerstone as the new font.

You cannot type in the preview area when you are in preview mode. When you are in preview mode, the Preview button changes to an Edit button. Click on the Edit button to return to the text box where you can type any changes to the text.

4. Click on the arrow next to the Size box and choose a font size of 24 to replace 30. This size change is also previewed when you're in preview mode.

The text preview box is not the same size as the actual text block on the sign. The preview area does, however, display the text as it will appear in the text block based on the current size, font, and style. You can, of course, change the size of the text block when you return to the main project window if you need to make room for more text.

5. Click on the arrow next to the Color box and select another color. If you're working in color on-screen, you'll note that the current color is yellow. Since our page color is a dark blue (we noted this when we opened the project), we'll need a light color. Select light gray for this example. The color does not change the style of the letter, but it does have an impact on the overall look of the sign. (The color change will not be previewed. When you're working on text in the Edit text dialog box, the text is always black in preview.)

You can change the style of the text, making it bold or italic or adding a shadow or a mask. A mask places a white outline around the text. This is useful for making the text stand out when it's a dark color on a dark background. Underlining, another style option, adds emphasis to a word without having an impact on the basic letter design. Experiment with these styles to see how they affect the text.

6. When you've finished looking at style options, select M (for mask).

Here's another option. You can justify the text within the text block, choosing between aligning the text to the left margin of the block, to the right edge, or to the center horizontally. You can also justify the text vertically, to the top edge, to the bottom, or to the center.

7. Select Center for both the horizontal and the vertical justification.

8. Everything looks good, so click on OK to return to the main project window, where we'll try making further attribute changes using the text toolbar.

 There are two other important options in the Edit Text dialog box: List Merge and Quotes and Verses, but don't worry about either of these just now. The list merge commands are covered extensively in Chapter 11, "Creating and Merging Lists," and we'll cover Quotes and Verses later in this chapter.

Using the Text Bar

A great way to change text attributes in the main project window is to use the text bar, shown below. The text bar is located just below the toolbar and is the place to do the final tweaking of the text attributes. It cannot be used to add to or change the text itself; you must use the Edit Text dialog box to do this.

You can make all the text changes available in the Edit Text dialog box using the text bar. The big advantage to using the text bar is that you can see the changes right on the project and you have the full array of the other PSD Ensemble II tools readily available in the main menu and submenus.

Keep in mind that whatever changes you make using the text bar will be applied to the entire text in the selected text block. If you want to change just some of the text or if you want to add more text, you will have to go back to the Edit Text dialog box.

The text bar is available only when you are editing a text block or a word balloon. It cannot be used for headlines, title blocks, or signature blocks. To edit these, you'll need to go into their separate dialog boxes, covered later in this chapter.

Let's change our text just a bit with the text bar.

1. If it's not still selected from before, select the text block that begins *Bring your old....* Notice that all options on the text bar become dark in color, indicating that they are available.

2. Click on the arrow beside the font box and change Cornerstone to Boulder. All the text in the block changes to the new font.

3. Click on each one of the eight alignment buttons on the text bar to see the effect each has on the text:

Button	Aligns text
	To the left
	Centered horizontally
	To the right
	Justified horizontally

Button	Aligns text
	To the top
	Centered vertically
	To the bottom
	Justified vertically

4. Change the size of the type to 40 and see how it becomes too big to fit in the text box.

5. Click on the bold, italic, and underline buttons to see how your text changes.

6. Click on shadow to add a drop shadow, then click on mask to put the mask back around the letters.

As you have now discovered, the text bar is great for making last-minute changes or for making changes that you want to see against the entire project; it can save you a lot of time.

Now let's take a look at what we can do with headlines.

◆ Working with Headlines

The headline is the most important part of almost all graphic presentations, so getting it just right can sometimes be a lengthy process. Fortunately, PSD Ensemble II gives you powerful tools to make great headlines. You can access these tools in the Headline dialog box, which is reached by double-clicking on a headline placeholder or by selecting the headline, then selecting Object ➤ Edit.

Let's make some improvements to the headline in the ready-made sign titled Jazz Festival, shown here. Open the Jazz Festival sign as follows:

1. Select File ➤ New (do not save changes) ➤ Signs & Posters ➤ Ready Made ➤ Community ➤ Jazz Festival. The Jazz Festival sign opens in the main project window.

2. Double-click on the headline *Fall Jazz Festival* to open the Headline dialog box, shown in Figure 10.3. You can also get to this dialog box by clicking once to select the headline, then selecting Object ➤ Edit. Here you can change the font, style, and color of the type, add various customized effects to the type, and select from a variety of headline designs.

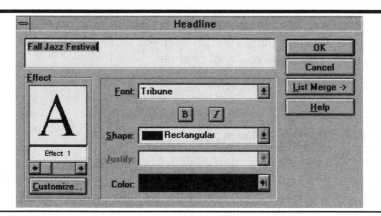

Figure 10.3:   The Headline dialog box opens with all the existing text selected.

When it is first opened, the Headline dialog box defaults to highlighting all of the copy in the text box. As in the Edit Text dialog box, all the highlighted text will be affected by any changes you make. If you want to change only a part of the text, select just that text. Remember that when text is selected, it can be erased by hitting any numeric or alphabetic key.

 You cannot change the size of the type in a headline. The type expands or contracts to fill the headline box. If you want smaller type, make the headline box smaller. If you want larger type, make the box larger. See "Resizing Headline or Text Blocks" in Chapter 2 for instructions.

Changing Headline Text Attributes

Let's make a few changes to make the Jazz Festival headline more exciting.

1. With the headline selected, make the type bold by clicking on the B button. The large *A* in the Effect box will change to reflect your selection. If you want to see the effect on the actual headline, you need to click OK and return to the main project window. We'll do that in a moment.

2. We think the headline would be more effective if it were on two lines. Place your cursor at the end of the word *Jazz* and press Enter. The headline splits into two lines and the Justify box now says Left, meaning that both Jazz and Festival are left-aligned. (Left is the default.)

3. Click on OK to return to the main project window to see the changes you've made so far. Shown here is the headline as it was

 when we opened the project and as it is now. Although we have not changed the font, the type looks different. In addition to making the text bold, we changed the headline to two lines instead of one; this caused the type to stretch in order to fit the headline box. It now looks thicker and bolder.

4. The left justification of the headline is making the second line of text seem off somehow, so let's change  this. Again, double-click on the headline to return to the Headline dialog box. In the Justify box, note your choices: Left, Center, Right, and Full, all shown here. (The difference between Full and Center is that Full stretches the lines to touch both left and right edges, while Center pushes them to the center.) Change the justification to Full, so that both lines stretch from edge to edge.

Your headline should now be split into two lines, fully justified, and bold. Now that we have the text attributes chosen, let's take a look at headline shapes.

Choosing a Headline Shape

The Shape option in the Headline dialog box offers you 21 different headline shapes. Let's take a look.

1. The headline in Jazz Festival is currently rectangular. Click on the Shape box to access the full list available. Each time you select a new shape, you'll have to click OK to return to the project window in order to see the new shape. All 21 possibilities are shown in Figure 10.4. As you can see, each of these shapes gives the project a totally different look.

2. When you're done experimenting with shapes, reopen the Headline dialog box and choose Round Top for the headline shape.

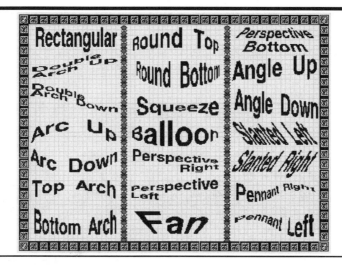

Figure 10.4: Choose your headline shape from these 21 different options.

3. Click on OK and take a look at the new headline shape in the project, shown here.

4. Double-click on the headline once again to access the Headline dialog box. Next we'll take a look at the text inside the headline.

Customizing Headline Text

On the left side of the Headline dialog box is a capital letter *A* with a sliding bar and a Customize button under it. If you slide the bar, you can choose from 25 preset text effects, labeled Effect 1, Effect 2, and so on. The last effect says only *Custom Effect*. This is the current effect—one you created, the default effect or, in this case, the ready-made effect. As you slide to each effect, the A changes to show that effect. If you click on the Customize button, you are offered the opportunity to design your own effect in the Custom Effect dialog box, shown in Figure 10.5.

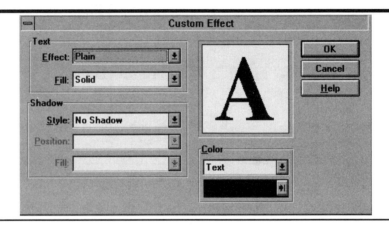

Figure 10.5: You can customize your text with outlines, shadows, and color blends using the Custom Effect dialog box.

Let's add an outline around all the text in the Jazz Festival headline.

1. Click on the Customize button to open the Custom Effect dialog box.

2. In the Text area of the Custom Effect dialog box, you can designate  a text effect of plain, thin outline, thick outline, or highlighted (these were illustrated under "Designing an Initial Cap" in Chapter 7). You can also select a text fill of solid, blend across, blend down, radiant, or double blend, as shown here. Select these options one by one to see what effect they have on the letter A in the preview window. When you're done experimenting, select a thick outline and a solid fill.

You can also add a shadow to your headline text, choosing its style, position, fill, and color. In the Shape box you can choose to have no shadow, or a drop shadow, block shadow, or silhouette (these were also illustrated in Chapter 7). If you select a shadow, you can choose its position relative to the letter—upper-right, upper-left, lower-right, or lower-left—from the Position list. If you select a silhouette as your shadow style, you can blend two colors with blend across, blend down, radiant, and double blend options in the Fill box. Keep in mind that this is a silhouette option, not a text option—the silhouette is the area immediately behind the text, not the text itself.

3. Experiment with the shadow options to see what effect they have on the letter *A* in the preview window. When you're done, select No Shadow.

4. The Color area lets you select the item you want to color and then designate a color. Your can choose the color for the text, text blend (if you select one of the fill options), outline (if you select thin or thick outline), shadow (if you select a shadow), and shadow blend

(if you choose to blend two colors into the shadow). Again, experiment as you will, and when you're done choose green for the text and blue for the outline.

5. Click on OK to return to the Headline dialog box, then click OK again to apply the changes to the headline in the main project window. Take a look at the final creation, shown here.

As with all creative pursuits, whether the sign is actually improved by our headline changes is a matter of personal taste. Feel free to make whatever changes you think look best.

NOTE   Like the Edit Text dialog box, the Headline dialog box has a List Merge button. We'll cover the list merge options in Chapter 11, "Creating and Merging Lists."

◆ Working with Title Blocks

A title block is a combination of a headline and one to two lines of regular text. These blocks can add a great deal of interest to your design, drawing attention to a sign, award, or banner. Title blocks are often used in documents where you need more than one line but want one of the lines to be dominant.

Choosing Type Styles for Title Blocks

There are only four available headline shapes in title blocks, compared to the 21 available for regular headlines. In title blocks, you can choose rectangular, arch up, squeeze, or top arch.

The second line in a title block is sized in relationship to the headline: small headline over large second line, medium over medium, or large over small. Headlines must be one line of up to 30 characters. Secondary lines can be one or two lines of up to 59 characters total (a return counts as a character).

The Title Block dialog box, shown in Figure 10.6, is divided into two parts, the Title Line (or headline) area and the Secondary Lines area. Both areas have font and text color options. Each area has type style options: bold or italic for the title line and bold, italic, underline, mask, and shadow for secondary lines. In addition, the Title Line area lets you select the headline shape and the size of the headline in relation to the secondary lines.

 Neither section of the Title Block dialog box offers specific text size options. As you remember, a headline will size to fit its box, and the secondary line is sized in relation to the headline.

Customizing a Title

The Title Block dialog box also has a Customize button that opens the Custom Effect dialog box. This dialog box has all the same options as the one for headlines and all the results look the same.

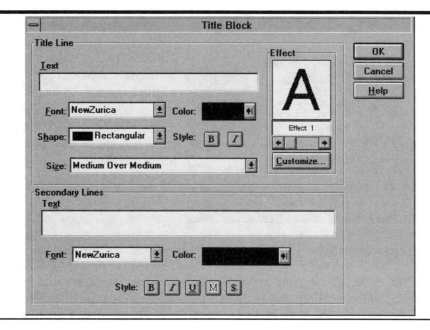

Figure 10.6: The Title Block dialog box is divided into two separate areas, one for the title line and one for the secondary lines.

◆ Adding a Signature Block

If you want to have an official signature on projects such as a certificate or an official note, you can add a signature block. Signature blocks come in seven different sizes and configurations that include from one to four signatures. You can even combine blocks if necessary to make larger blocks of signatures.

Signature blocks are designed so that you enter text to appear under a signature line, with the area above the line left blank for a signature when you print it out. If you like, you can spice up a project by adding special Print Shop autographs of famous people such as George Washington. Only PSD autographs will appear above the signature line. A line with no chosen PSD autograph will remain blank.

Selecting a Block Type

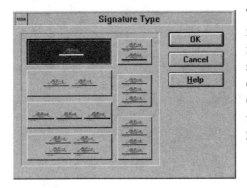

The seven sizes and configurations for signature blocks are available in the Signature Type dialog box, shown here. You can access this dialog box by clicking on the Object menu or the New Object tool and selecting Add ➤ Signature Block.

Let's select a style and create a signature block of our own.

1. Select File ➤ New ➤ No ➤ Signs & Posters ➤ Start From Scratch, and then hold down Ctrl while you click on Wide as your orientation. You arrive at a blank page in the main project window.

2. Select Object ➤ Add ➤ Signature Block. The Signature Type dialog box opens.

3. Select the block with two signatures side by side and click on OK.

4. The selected signature lines are placed on the center of the page.

You can change to another signature block at any time if you decide you need more or fewer signatures: just double-click on the signature lines to open the Edit Signature Block dialog box (we'll see this next), then click on the Change button. The Signature Type dialog box will reopen and you can select another style. If you choose fewer signatures than you had in your first choice, the lines will be deleted from the bottom up as listed in the Edit Signature Block dialog box. This is important to remember if you've already entered text into any of the signature blocks.

Now let's look at text options for signature lines.

Choosing Text Attributes for Signature Lines

The Edit Signature Block dialog box, shown in Figure 10.7, lets you designate what will appear in the signature block, as well as what it will look

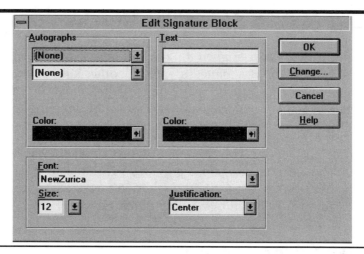

Figure 10.7: The Edit Signature Block dialog box lets you insert a famous autograph, add text below signature lines, and designate text attributes.

like. You can access it by double-clicking on the signature block or by selecting the signature block and choosing Object ➤ Edit ➤ Signature Block. This dialog box has three sections, one part for PSD autographs (which we'll explain below), another where you can type the text to appear under the signature lines, and a third for attributes of the text under the lines.

Note that Figure 10.7 shows two boxes in both the Autographs section and the Text section of the dialog box; this is because we selected a signature block with two signature lines earlier. If we had selected one signature line, one box would appear in each section; three lines would produce three boxes in each section; and so on.

You can add a PSD autograph to appear on top of each line, or you can type in text to appear below each line. You can also choose the color for the autographs and the text under the signature lines.

The Justification box gives you various options for justifying the text below the signature lines. These options change based on the configuration of your signature block. For stacked signatures, you can choose Left, Right, Center, or Full. For side-by-side signatures, your choices will be Left, Center, Right, Full, or Left/Right. (Left/Right left-aligns text under the left signature line and right-aligns text under the right signature line.)

Adding Text to Signature Blocks

Signature blocks are designed for a line of text below the signature line where you can insert a name, title, or any other kind of text. To enter the text, simply place your cursor in one of the text boxes in the Text section of the Edit Signature Block dialog box and start typing. The signature text lines can accommodate up to 30 characters.

As mentioned above, you cannot enter text above the signature line except through the autographs provided with the PSD program. We'll cover these in the next section. If you don't use a PSD autograph, the line is automatically left blank for a signature.

Inserting Autographs

The PSD Ensemble II program provides you with 38 autographs that you can add to spice up your documents. You can insert them into any signature block by selecting them from the drop-down lists in the Autographs section of the Edit Signature Block dialog box. PSD Ensemble II has persuaded the following VIPs to allow you to use their autographs in your projects:

A. Lincoln	F. Nightingale	R. Bonheur
B. Franklin	G. Washington	Rembrandt
Bear Paw	Geronimo	S.B. Anthony
C. Darwin	H.C. Anderson	Santa Claus
C. Dickens	Isaac Newton	Sitting Bull
Carmen Sandiego	J. Hancock	The Chief
Cat Paw	J. Muir	The President
Charlemagne	Joan of Arc	Thumbprint
D. Boone	L. Pasteur	Tooth Fairy
Dog Paw	L.V. Beethoven	W. Clark
Easter Bunny	Leonardo	W. Shakespeare
Elizabeth I	Mark Twain	W.A. Mozart
Emily Dickinson	Michelangelo	

Let's change the signature block type, add some text, insert an auto-graph, and make some changes to the text attributes. You should still be in the main project window with two stacked signatures on the page.

1. Double-click on the signature lines to open the Edit Signature Block dialog box.

2. Click on the Change button, select the signature block with four signatures in two rows of two, and click on OK.

3. Double-click on the signature lines to open the Edit Signature Block dialog box again.

4. In the Autographs section, click on the arrow next to the first text box and select A. Lincoln from the drop-down list that appears. The name *A. Lincoln* now appears in the first box in both the Auto-graphs section and the Text section of the dialog box.

5. Type your own name into the second text box under Text, right under A. Lincoln's.

6. Select dark gray as the color of the autograph from the Color box under Autographs.

7. Select black as the color of the text from the Color box under Text.

8. In the Size box at the bottom, change the type size to 26. Leave the font as it is.

9. Click on OK to return to the main project window. The signature block now contains A. Lincoln's autograph in dark gray and the typed A. Lincoln and your name in black, as shown here. The line above your name is blank, awaiting your signature.

> _A. Lincoln_   _J.R. Caruso_

Looks good, but we still have two blank lines. We could go to the dialog box again and add more signatures, but instead let's delete those two extra signature lines.

10. Double-click on the signature lines to access the Edit Signature Block dialog box.

11. Click on Change. The Signature Type box pops up. Select the block with two signatures, one on top of the other, and click OK. We're back to two signature lines.

12. Select the signature block and click on the Delete tool or hit the Delete key on your keyboard. The signature block disappears and you once again have a blank page.

Now let's take a look at text in a word balloon.

◆ Adding a Word Balloon

Word balloons are an interesting way to add text to your projects. There are 15 word balloon shapes available, as shown in the Word Balloon Type dialog box in Figure 10.8.

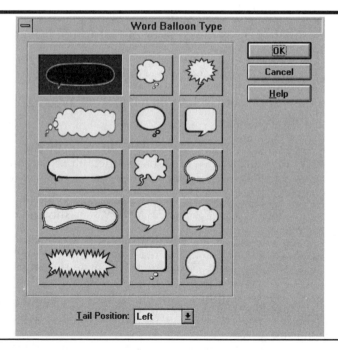

Figure 10.8:   Word balloons come in many different shapes.

Let's add a word balloon to our blank page.

1. Select Object ➤ Add ➤ Word Balloon or click on the Object tool and select Word Balloon. The Word Balloon Type dialog box pops up.

2. Click on the balloon in the lower-right corner.

3. You can choose to have the tail of the word balloon pointing to the left, centered, or pointing to the right, as shown here, by clicking on your choice in the Tail Position drop-down list at the bottom of the dialog box. Select Right and click on OK to return to the main project window.

The tail position of a word balloon varies depending on its original design in the Select a Balloon Type dialog box. For example, if the tail starts in the center position in this dialog box, the tail will shift only slightly left and right. If the tail points far left in the dialog box, it will point far right when you select Right as the tail position and will be centered when you select Center.

Once you've added a word balloon to your project, you'll want to add text to it.

1. Double-click on the word balloon or select it and click on Object ➤ Edit. The Edit Word Balloon Text dialog box, shown in Figure 10.9, opens. This dialog box works just like the Edit Text dialog box with one exception: it has a Change Shape button. If you click on this button, you return to the Word Balloon Type dialog box, where you can change to an entirely different balloon.

2. Try adding some text to your word balloon. Type **I love PSD Ensemble II. It's great stuff!** Note that word balloons, like text

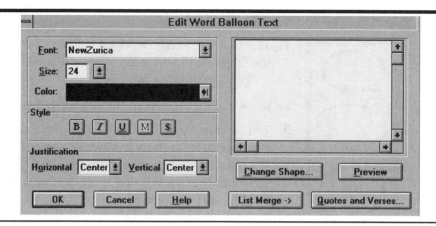

Figure 10.9: The Edit Word Balloon Text dialog box offers you the same options as the Edit Text box, with the addition of the Change Shape button.

blocks, have no limit to the amount of text that can be entered. As long as it fits on the page, you can add text. Also like text blocks, if the text is bigger than the area of the word balloon, the text that doesn't fit will be hidden from sight.

3. When you're finished entering text, click on OK to return to the main project window.

4. Resize the balloon until you can see all the text, as shown here.

5. Since a word balloon implies a speaker, insert an appropriate graphic. We've chosen Carmen Sandiego from the Carmen Squares library.

The Edit Word Balloon Text dialog box includes a List Merge button and a Quotes and Verses button, making both of these options available to insert into your word balloon. See Chapter 11 for information about merging lists, and see "Exploring Quotes and Verses" later in this chapter for information about those elements.

Keep this document open; we'll use it again to try out our next type of text block.

◆ Exploring Quotes and Verses

PSD Ensemble II offers over 200 quotes and verses for customizing your projects. Some quotes and verses are divided into two separate locations, designated as (1) and (2). These divided quotes and verses are designed to be inserted on different pages of a project or in different areas of the project. The first part is an opening line for the front of a greeting card. The second part completes the thought and is designed for the inside of a greeting card.

Let's try adding a quote to the word balloon we created above.

1. Click on the word balloon to open the Edit Word Balloon Text dialog box. Delete the text you have there now.

2. Click on the Quotes and Verses button.

The Quotes and Verses Browser, shown in Figure 10.10, pops up. This browser works like the Graphics Browser, the Backdrops Browser, and the Borders Browser; it shows the verse names on the left and the full text of the verses in the preview window.

If you wanted to add a quote or verse to a text block, you would double-click on the text block to open the Edit Text dialog box, and then click on the Quotes and Verses button there. Quotes and Verses are not available from any other source in PSD Ensemble II.

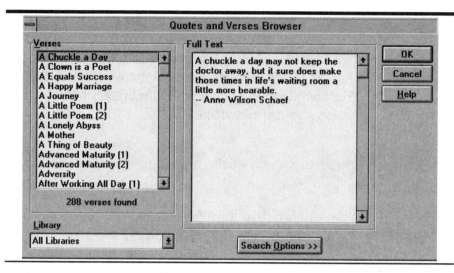

Figure 10.10: The Quotes and Verses Browser dialog box shows verse names on the left and the full text on the right.

There is only one library of quotes and verses. If you select All Libraries, you get the same quotes and verses that you get when you select the Quotes and Verses Library.

3. As with the other browsers, you can use the search options to conduct a search for the right verse. Click on the Search Options button, then on the Category Keywords button to bring up the Category Keywords dialog box, shown here. The selections are

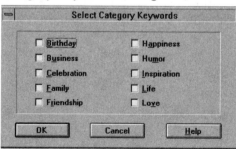

more limited than on the other browser dialog boxes, since you are dealing here with a concept rather than a tangible graphic. In other words, you want an inspirational message of love rather than a burger-eating dinosaur.

4. In the Category Keywords box, check the Humor box and click on OK.

5. Click on the Search button to search the library for humor-related quotes and verses. This search produces more than 150 choices.

6. Click on *Are we having fun yet?*, then click on OK to return to the Edit Word Balloon Text dialog box. Here you can make changes to the type, including style and color. You can also edit the text of the quote or verse.

7. Highlight the quote and change the font to Scribble.

8. Highlight *Carol Burnett*, change the type size to 20 and click on the M button to add a mask to the name.

9. When you're satisfied with your work, click on OK; the text is added to your project. If necessary, resize the word balloon so that all the text fits properly, as shown here. (We've chosen another Carmen Sandiego graphic to accompany the balloon.)

As already mentioned, some quotes and verses are divided into two parts that go together, designated (1) and (2). For example, Boat for Christmas (1) and Boat for Christmas (2) go together, as shown here.

And that's the end of word balloons and this chapter. Select File ➤ New and do not save your changes.

◆ Endnotes

That's everything you need to know about text and headlines. You know how to:

◆ Edit a text block, choose text attributes, and preview the text

◆ Use the text bar to change existing text in the main project window

◆ Turn text into outlined, shadowed, or silhouetted specialty text

◆ Add a signature block and get Mozart to sign it for you

◆ Animate a project with a word balloon and add a quote that you wish you'd said yourself

It's a lot to absorb, but as you work on projects, you will become accustomed to all these options and eventually they'll seem simple. You're a text whiz and now you're ready to tackle Chapter 11, "Creating and Merging Lists."

Chapter 11
Chapter 11
Chapter 11
Chapter 11
Chapter 11
Chapter 11

Chapter Eleven

Creating and Merging Lists

Your mission: to create and merge name lists

◆

You can use Print Shop's Name List feature to create and merge all kinds of lists. PSD Ensemble II name lists come in two different types: address lists and custom lists.

Address lists, as the name implies, are specifically for names and addresses. This is where you'd create a mailing list of your best customers or a Christmas card list of friends and family. Custom lists can be virtually anything, from a list of your favorite CDs to a list of movies you'd like to rent.

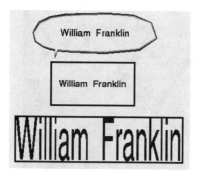

Merging information from lists into projects is a great way to add a personal touch. You can merge lists into any project through a word balloon, a text block, or a headline block, all shown here.

Let's take a look at how lists are created.

◆ Creating Lists

Creating a list is as simple as typing in the information. Once the information has been created and stored, you can access it at any time and bring it into a project.

Address lists are created in the Address List dialog box, and custom lists are created in the Custom List dialog box. You can access these dialog boxes in one of two ways:

- ◆ From the Select a Project dialog box, choose Extras ➤ Name Lists ➤ Address List or Custom List.

- ◆ From the main project window, choose Extras ➤ Edit Address List or Edit Custom List.

The Address List or Custom List dialog box will open. To start a new list, click on File ➤ New. If you want to make changes or additions to an existing list, click on File ➤ Open and select the file you want to work on.

Making an Address List

To create an address list, just fill in the blanks in the Address List dialog box, shown in Figure 11.1. The Filename section at the top of the dialog box says "Untitled.DAT," meaning that this is a brand new address list that has not yet been given a name.

Address List

File

Filename: Untitled.DAT

Name List Entry:

First name: Last name:

Address line 1:

Address line 2:

City: State: Zip:

Other:

OK

Cancel

Help

Add Entry

Delete Entry

Figure 11.1: The Address List dialog box is designed to store a complete address.

The Name List Entry box near the top of the dialog box shows the first entry in the current address list. Since we haven't created any entries yet, this box is empty in Figure 11.1. Once you have created a list, you can click on the arrow to the right of the box to access an alphabetical drop-down list of entries.

The Address List dialog box provides eight information boxes for each entry. Type the relevant information into each text box. The maximum number of characters per text box is as follows:

Text box	Number of characters
First Name	20
Last Name	20
Address line 1	60
Address line 2	60
City	20

Text box	Number of characters
State	2
Zip	10
Other	60

 Use Tab to move down the dialog box from one text box to the next. Use Shift+Tab to move up through the boxes. You can also use your mouse to move from box to box.

You do not have to fill in all the boxes for every entry, but you must fill in the Last Name box because Address Lists are stored alphabetically by the last name. If you fail to put a name in the Last Name line and try to move on, the pop-up prompt shown here reminds you that you must enter a name or lose the entry.

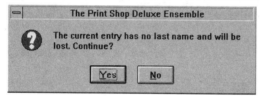

 If you are creating an address list of company names rather than individuals, you can type the name of the company in the Last Name line and nothing in the First Name line, or you can split the company name to fill both the First Name and Last Name lines. If you split the name, remember that the list will be arranged alphabetically based on what is entered in the Last Name line.

Let's create an address list with several entries.

1. From the Select a Project dialog box, select Extras ➤ Name Lists ➤ Address List; the Address List dialog box appears.

2. Type the name and address of a friend in the appropriate boxes. Put your friend's nickname in the Other box.

3. When you've completed the address record, click on Add Entry. The entry disappears and a new, blank Address List dialog box appears.

4. The arrow next to the Name List Entry box is now dark, indicating that there is something hidden from view. Click on this arrow and your friend's name appears, last name first. The title of an address list entry is always whatever you entered in the last name box followed by what you entered in the first name box. Click on the name and the complete entry for your friend is again on-screen. You can edit or delete it altogether.

5. Click on Add Entry again. Your friend's name is again stored and the blank entry form appears again.

6. Type a new entry for another friend. When you're finished, click on Add Entry again.

7. Repeat the process for a third friend.

 Every address list or custom list file can include up to 200 entries, and you can create an unlimited number of address or custom lists.

8. Click on OK, and a prompt asks if you want to save your work.

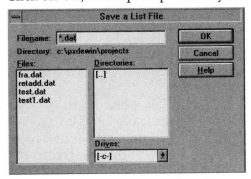

Click OK and the Save a List File dialog box appears, as shown here. Type **red** in the Filename box (the extension .dat will be added automatically) and click on OK. You return to the Select a Project dialog box.

Now that you've saved the list, you can open it at any time in one of two ways:

◆ From the Select a Project dialog box, choose Extras ➤ Name Lists ➤ Address List. In the Address List dialog box, select File ➤ Open and choose red.dat from the list that appears.

◆ From the main project window, select Extras ➤ Edit Address List. In the Address List dialog box, select File ➤ Open and choose red.dat from the list that appears.

9. Create another address list of at least two entries. Follow the same steps you followed to create the red file. Call this second list *green*. We'll use both of these lists when we merge a list into a document later in this chapter.

 If you want to create an address or custom list that includes many entries from another list, open the existing list file, as noted above, and use the Save As command from the File menu to save it under a different name. Then open the second file and customize it to your liking.

When you've finished creating your green address list, you should be at the Select a Project dialog box, ready to make a custom list.

Making a Custom List

As with address lists, all you have to do to create an entry in a custom list is fill in the blanks in the Custom List dialog box, shown in Figure 11.2. The information boxes in this dialog box are labeled simply Line 1, 2, 3, 4, and 5. The maximum number of characters per line is 60.

Let's start a custom list of our favorite movies. We can use this list to print labels, among other things.

1. From the Select a Project dialog box, select Extras ➤ Name Lists ➤ Custom List. The Custom List dialog box pops up. (You could also reach this dialog box from the main project window by clicking on the Extras menu and selecting Edit Custom List.)

2. In the Line 1 box, type **Casablanca**. You must always have an entry in Line 1. You do not need to have an entry in any other box.

3. Fill in the rest of the boxes as follows:

Line 2	**102 minutes, black and white**
Line 3	**Humphrey Bogart, Ingrid Bergman**
Line 4	**Sydney Greenstreet, Peter Lorre**
Line 5	**Rick's Cafe Americain, "As Time Goes By"**

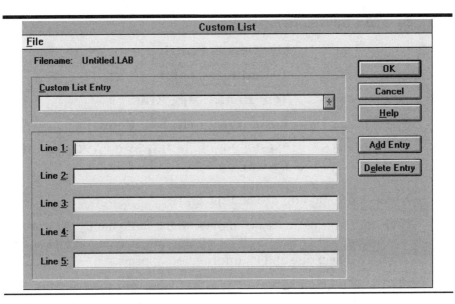

Figure 11.2:   The Custom List dialog box offers five lines in which to enter whatever information you wish.

4. Click on Add Entry. As before, the entry disappears and the arrow next to the Custom List Entry box turns dark, indicating that there is an entry hidden from view.

5. Click on the arrow and a drop-down list shows a Casablanca entry. The title of a custom list entry is always whatever you entered in the Line 1 box.

6. Add a second Custom List entry as follows:

Line 1	**Dr. No**
Line 2	**112 minutes, color**
Line 3	**Sean Connery, Ursula Andress**
Line 4	**Joseph Wiseman, Jack Lord**
Line 5	**007, Miss Moneypenny, Honey, M, Puss-Feller**

7. Click on Add Entry.

8. Add a third Custom List entry:

Line 1	**Sleepless in Seattle**
Line 2	**105 minutes, color**
Line 3	**Tom Hanks, Meg Ryan**
Line 4	**Rosie O'Donnell, Rob Reiner**
Line 5	**"Make Someone Happy," "A Kiss to Build a Dream On"**

9. Click on Add Entry to add the entry.

10. Before storing this list of movies under a file name, click on Custom List Entry. You'll see all the movies listed in alphabetical order. Select one and its information appears.

11. Click on OK, and a prompt asks if you want to save your changes. Click on OK, and the Save a List file dialog box appears. Type **movies** and click on OK. The program will automatically add the extension *lab*. Once you've saved the file, you will be back at the Select a Project dialog box.

You have created a custom list with three entries. You can open it at any time in one of two ways:

◆ From the main project window, select Extras ➤ Edit Custom List. In the Custom List dialog box, select File ➤ Open ➤ movies.lab.

◆ From the Select a Project dialog box, select Extras ➤ Name Lists ➤ Custom List. In the Custom List dialog box, select File ➤ Open ➤ movies.lab.

◆ Modifying Lists

Name lists are easy to modify. All you need to do is open a list, select the entry you want to modify, and type the changes.

Let's open the *red* address list we created earlier in the chapter.

1. From the Select a Project dialog box, select Extras ➤ Name Lists ➤ Address List.

You may discover that the Address List dialog box has an entry in it. If it does, look at the Filename area at the top of the dialog box. You'll probably discover that the entry you see is the first alphabetical entry in the last address file you created. If you were trying to create a new address list, click New from the File menu on the Edit Address List dialog box. The entry disappears and the Filename area reads "Untitled." You are ready to begin a new list.

2. Click on the File menu and select Open. The Open File dialog box pops up.

3. Select red.dat and click on OK. The arrow next to the Name List Entry box becomes dark.

4. Click on the arrow and select one of your friends' names from the drop-down list of entries. This entry opens. Add another nickname to the Other text box and click on Add Entry.

If you want to delete an entry, select it from the Name List Entry box and click on the Delete Entry button; the entry disappears. There is no warning prompt, so be sure you want to delete the entry before you click on this button.

◆ Merging Lists

You create Print Shop name lists so that you can merge them into your projects using the Merge List command, to address envelopes, make labels, or personalize a project message. You can use the Merge List command with a text block, a word balloon or a headline block.

You can merge only one entry into a project at a time. In other words, you cannot merge Line 1 from the Casablanca entry and Line 1 from the Dr. No entry into the same project. If you try to do this by putting in two Line 1 merge commands, Print Shop will just repeat the entry selected first. In this case, the merge would read *Casablanca, Casablanca*, not *Casablanca, Dr. No*.

Merging a List into a Project

To merge a list into a project, you need to open a list file so you can see a preview of how the merged text will look in the project.

1. From the Select a Project dialog box, select Stationery ➤ Start From Scratch ➤ Envelopes ➤ Print Shop ➤ Bay Cruise Backdrop ➤ USPS Bay Cruise 1 Layout.

You arrive at the main project window with an envelope layout that includes one text block and one undesignated white rectangular box, as shown in Figure 11.3. Since this is an envelope, the text box must be for a name and address and the white rectangular box must be for a return address.

Return address boxes have no designation other than being white boxes. When they appear in USPS (United States Postal Service) layouts, they are specifically for the return address you enter in your PSD program. USPS layouts meet post office specifications and are available in postcard and envelope projects only.

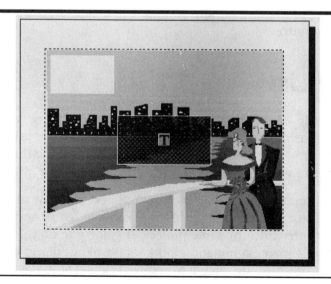

Figure 11.3:   The envelope project has a backdrop, a text placeholder, and an undesignated white rectangular box.

First, let's fill the return address box.

2. Click on the Extras menu and select Edit Return Address. The Return Address dialog box, shown in Figure 11.4, pops up.

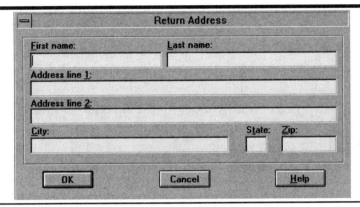

Figure 11.4:   The address you type into this Return Address dialog box will be placed automatically into all USPS envelope and postcard projects.

3. Type your return address in the appropriate text boxes.

4. Click on OK; you return to the main project window. Your return address is now inside the white box, as shown here.

From here on, this return address will appear in return address boxes automatically. You will never have to type it again. If you want to change it, return to the Return Address dialog box and type in the changes. Print Shop can store only one return address at a time.

Choosing a List to Merge

Let's select a list to merge into this project.

1. Click on the Extras menu again and select Edit Address List from the options offered. The Address List dialog box pops up.

2. Click on the File menu and select Open. The Open a List File dialog box pops up, listing all the address list files available.

3. Select red.dat and click OK. The red address list opens and the first alphabetical entry appears in the Address List dialog box.

4. Click OK to return to the main project window.

5. Click on the Extras menu once again, then click on Select List Type. You'll see a check mark next to Address List, indicating that it has been selected.

 If you prefer, you can wait until after you have selected your merge fields (see the next section) to select the file to merge into.

Selecting Merge Fields

Now we're ready to merge the *red* file into the project.

1. Double-click on the text placeholder. As usual, the Edit Text box appears.

2. Click on the List Merge button in the lower-right corner. A list of options that correspond to the information boxes in the Address

First Name
Last Name
Line 1 - Full Name
Line 2 - Address 1
Line 3 - Address 2
Line 4 - City, State, Zip
Line 5 - Other
All Lines

List dialog box pops up, as shown here. If you select an option, the corresponding merge field will appear in the text preview area of the Edit Text dialog box.

3. Choose the fields you want to include on the envelope: Full Name, Address 1, Address 2 (if you entered additional information in this box), City, State, and Zip. As you select each field, it is recorded as a separate line in the preview box.

4. Combine <line 2> and <line 3> (Address 1 and Address 2), as

<line 1>
<line 2>, <line 3>
<line 4>

shown here, by typing a comma after <line 2> and then pressing the Delete key to delete the return.

You can choose a font, type size, style, and color for a merge field in the Edit Text dialog box just as you would for any other text.

5. To see what will actually print on the envelope, click on the Preview button. The merge fields will be replaced by the name and address from the first entry in the selected address list, as shown here.

 Do not be concerned if you do not want the first person on the list to get this envelope. You will have the opportunity to select exactly who on this address list gets the mailing when you actually print the project.

6. Once all your merge commands are set in the preview window, click OK to return to the main project window. The envelope is now addressed to the first person on the address list and has your return address on it, as shown in Figure 11.5.

Now we just have to print the project.

Figure 11.5:   The envelope, complete with addressee and return address

◆ Printing a List

Print Shop knows that you have performed a list merge in this project because you have inserted merge fields. When you print the project, it will use entries from the active list unless you tell it differently. The Print command allows you to designate which entries from the active list you want to merge. You can even change the active list.

Let's give it a try. The envelope should still be open in the main project window.

1. Click on the File menu and select Print.

The Print dialog box, shown here, pops up. (Actually there are more options than shown here, but you don't need to worry about them for

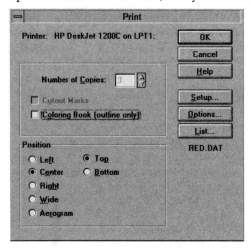

now. See "Printing Envelopes" in Chapter 12 for a complete explanation of envelope printing options.) Below the List button on the right side of the dialog box is the name of the list we selected earlier, red.dat. The Number of Copies box defaults to 3 because this is the number of entries in the red.dat file. The 3 is light gray, meaning that you cannot change it, at least not in this box.

If you want to print a copy of the project for every name in red.dat, you can just click on OK. If you want to select names from the list or change to another list, click on the List button. Let's change the recipients of the mailing.

2. Click on the List button. The Open a List File dialog box pops up. No file is selected, so click on red.dat.

3. Once you've selected a file, the List Entries button becomes available. Click on this button.

4. The Select List Entries dialog box, shown in Figure 11.6, pops up, listing all the entries in the *red* file. You can select the entries you want to include in this printing by clicking on them. If you want to deselect an entry, click on it again. If you decide to print all the entries after all, you can click on the All List Entries button at the bottom of the dialog box. For this example, select only one of the entries.

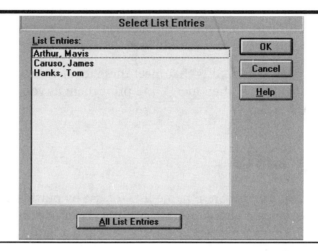

Figure 11.6: The Select List Entries dialog box shows all the entries in a file.

5. Click on OK. In the Open a List File dialog box, click OK again. The Print dialog box returns and now the Number of Copies says 1 because you have elected to print a copy of the project to only one name.

6. Click on OK to print the envelope.

It's that easy: create a list, open the project you want to merge into, add merge fields to a text block, headline block, or word balloon, and select which entries you want printed.

 See "Printing a Name List" in Chapter 12 for more information on dealing with problems you might encounter when you print using a list merge.

◆ Importing Lists

PSD Ensemble II lets you open lists created in other programs and merge them into Print Shop projects, provided these lists meet certain requirements. They must be saved as ASCII files, the fields within each entry must be separated by a tab, and every entry must be separated by a hard carriage return.

In addition, the entries in the files must meet all the specifications listed above relating to the number of characters per line, the number of lines included, and the order of the lines.

You can open outside lists that meet these requirements from the Open a List File dialog box, then merge and print them as you would a Print Shop list.

◆ Exporting Lists

You can export Print Shop name lists for use by outside programs that use the same type of file format. PSD lists are tab-delimited ASCII files, with a tab character separating every field and a hard carriage return separating every entry.

Let's try exporting a file. We're going to bring the file into Word for Windows but you could also do it in another program. The list file is fine the way it is. You do not need to change it or resave it at all.

1. Open Word.

2. Select File ➤ New and choose Normal as your format.

3. Click on Insert ➤ File.

4. Navigate to the PSDEWIN Projects file and select red.dat.

5. Click on OK and the entire list is imported into the Word document.

If you find searching for the file in PSDEWIN too time consuming, save the list to a different directory, for example, c:\word\psd\red.dat. This way when you insert the list into the word file, you can get it from the Word directory.

◆ Endnotes

That's everything you need to know about name lists. Now you know:

- ◆ How to create an address list or a custom list
- ◆ How to open, start, and save a list
- ◆ How to modify or delete an entry in a list
- ◆ How to merge a list into a project and how to select and choose which entries from the list get printed on the project
- ◆ What a USPS format is and why you need it

Most important, you know how easy it is to create and merge lists. Now on to Chapter 12, "Printing Made Easy."

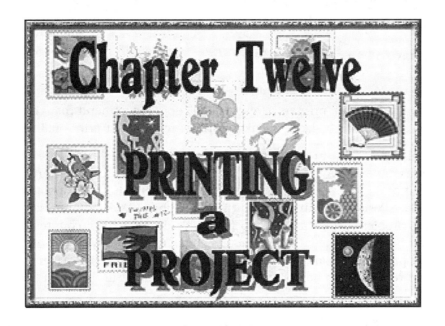

Printing Made Easy

Your mission: to learn tips for printing specific projects and solving printing problems

◆

Throughout the course of this book we've printed various projects and gotten a good idea of the basics of printing. This chapter will give some tips for printing specific projects. If you need a review of all the print options Print Shop offers, see the "Choosing Preferences" and "Printing a Project" sections of Chapter 3.

There's nothing more frustrating than discovering that one of your great projects just does not print right. PSD Ensemble II supports most printers that are supported by Microsoft Windows 3.1 or Windows 95, including

9-pin dot matrix printers. However, PSD does recommend that you use a 24-pin dot matrix, laser, or ink jet printer for the best print quality.

Many of the print problems you do encounter will be due to the limitations of your own printer. Maybe you're asking it to do something it just cannot do. For example, a monochrome printer cannot print color and only a PostScript printer will print EPS graphics. Aside from these obvious problems, there are other print problems you may encounter that can be solved. The latter part of this chapter will deal with troubleshooting printing to make it easier for you to take that great on-screen project and turn it into a hard copy you can post on the wall or pop in the mail.

◆ Printing Specific Projects

Some projects print differently than others because they're a unique size or a distinct orientation. These projects include banners, which print on multiple pages, name lists, which are imported into projects piece by piece, labels, which repeat over and over on a specific area of a page, and business cards, which print 8 to 10 per page.

Printing Banners

Banners are multipage, from a minimum of 3 pages to as many as 35. They can be printed on a tractor-fed (continuous) printer or a cut-sheet (one page at a time) printer.

If you're printing on a cut-sheet printer, you will need to glue or tape the pages together. To put the pages together seamlessly, carefully trim one side, then use glue on the exposed side and transparent tape on the underside. PSD Ensemble II suggests that you glue the pages together first and apply the tape to the underside after all the pieces are assembled to your liking.

If you're printing on a dot matrix printer, you may experience some problems with overheating, especially if you're printing a particularly long banner. Overheating can damage the print heads, so be careful. Some printers will shut down automatically if they become overheated, but don't count on this. It's a good idea to stop printing after several minutes to give the printer a breather, just to be on the safe side. You can start again after the printer cools.

If you're having difficulties using a tractor-fed printer, use the Cut sheet banner printing option in the Preferences dialog box to tell the program to treat the printer like a cut-sheet printer, as discussed in Chapter 3.

Banners can be printed in a coloring book format. This option prints the banner in outline form, a good way to check the layout before final printing. Also, you might want to use this option and then color in your banner just for fun.

Printing Name Lists

Merge printing with name lists is generally a breeze. The one problem you might confront is cutoff of some of the merged text. This is generally due to the size of the box in which the text is placed. To solve the problem, make sure that the text block, headline block, or word balloon where the merged text will be placed is large enough to accommodate the largest of the merged text.

For example, if you're merging names and addresses, the third name on the list may be longer than the first, so what initially appeared to be a big enough space really isn't. Just resize the text box to make it large enough for this longer name to fit, and you will have no more problems with cutoff.

Printing Labels

When you select File ➤ Print, the number of labels to be printed on a page is indicated in the Print dialog box. The number of labels printed on a page is determined by the type of label you select. Label size is the very first thing you select when you begin a Label project.

Labels print in multiples on one page, so it is critical that each one fits properly within its assigned space. If one prints outside its assigned area, it will throw off all the others and your labels will be worthless.

You need to keep this in mind while you're designing the label. Be sure to leave a safe area of white space around the design and text areas. This will help with any variation in placement. Also, the program automatically scales labels down to 99% of their original size when you print them to better ensure that each will fit into its designated space.

Before you print on pressure-sensitive labels or card stock, print one page of your labels on plain white paper. Then hold this paper up to the labels to see if they fit properly. If they don't, use the alignment options in the Print Options dialog box to try to solve the problem. If this doesn't work, try scaling the labels down to make them smaller than 99% so they will fit into their designated areas properly.

When you print labels you are offered an additional option in the Print dialog box: the Starting Place button. Click on this button to reach a dialog box, shown in Figure 12.1, that allows you to select where you want to start printing on a sheet of labels. This is particularly useful if you're not using a complete sheet of labels.

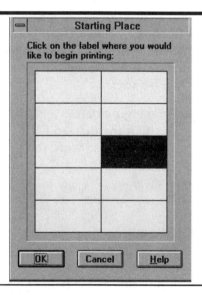

Figure 12.1:   The Starting Place dialog box lets you choose where on the label sheet you want to begin printing.

Printing Business Cards

Business cards print 10 to a page on most printers. Some printers that require a large *grab area* to feed in the paper print cards 8 to a page. Cards can be printed on regular paper and then photocopied onto card stock or, on some printers, you can print directly onto card stock.

If you're printing onto card stock, make sure your cards line up properly. Print a first page on plain paper and then check this against the card stock to make sure the cards are aligned properly.

Printing Envelopes

Envelope printing is tricky because it's not a full page-sized project and envelopes do not feed into the printer like regular pieces of paper do. When you select File ➤ Print for an envelope, the Print dialog box offers special Position options, which refer to how the envelopes are fed into your printer. The options are Left, Right, Center, Wide, and Aerogram for printer feed and Top and Bottom for the position of the printed text, as shown in Figure 12.2.

 An aerogram is a type of envelope used mainly for international letters. To create an aerogram, select Aerogram to print the envelope's address in the center of a regular sheet of paper. Turn the page over, feed it back into the printer, and print the message on the opposite side. Then fold the page in thirds so that the address side is out. Put a stamp on it and mail it.

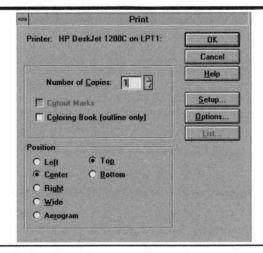

Figure 12.2: Position options for envelopes include Left, Right, Center, Wide, and Aerogram.

Most printers that feed envelopes left, center, or right print better with the position choice set to Bottom. Most printers that feed envelopes wide print better with the position choice set to Top.

Printers that feed wide may not be able to print all the way to the right edge and thus may not look centered. You cannot eliminate this problem but you can make it less obvious by not putting borders around your envelope design.

If you're still having problems printing, try using the Rotate envelope option in the Preferences dialog box, as discussed in the "Choosing Preferences" section of Chapter 3.

◆ Troubleshooting Print Problems

PSD Ensemble II provides some help on troubleshooting print problems in its extensive Help library (see Chapter 4, "Getting Help"). If you don't find your particular problem discussed here, check out Help for more information. In the meantime, here are two common problems you might encounter.

Dealing with Partial Printouts

If your printer is printing only part of your project, it may be that the printer does not have enough memory to store the entire project. Printer memory is separate from your computer's memory. If you don't know how much memory your printer has, check the printer manual to find out.

The higher the resolution at which you elect to print a project, the more memory you will need. For example, with a laser printer, you'll generally need 512K of printer memory to print at 150 dpi (dots per inch). At 300 dpi, you'll need 1MB. If you're having trouble printing, lower the resolution.

If lowering the dpi does not work, the printer may be *timing out* or it may have a third-party print spooler with a time out feature. When a printer times out, it begins to print what it has stored if it doesn't receive any new information within a certain number of seconds. This may prevent part of the project from being stored for printout. This problem can usually be resolved by turning off the time out feature or increasing its value to 90 seconds (see the printer manual for instructions).

Printing TrueType Fonts

The 73 TrueType Fonts used in PSD Ensemble II sometimes become pixelized when you print them out. The problem may be the resolution at which you print them; at less than 300 dpi, the print quality of TrueType fonts is less than perfect. If a printout looks funny to you, try printing it at a higher resolution.

Here is another problem that may occur with TrueType fonts in Windows: colored TrueType fonts in larger point sizes sometimes get mapped to a different color than the one you selected. Other fonts such as PostScript fonts are not affected by this problem. If your TrueType fonts are printing out the wrong color, try using a PostScript font. You can use PostScript Type 1 fonts in Print Shop by installing Adobe Type Manager for Windows.

◆ Endnotes

In this last chapter, you've learned about some print problems you might encounter and how to solve them. You now know:

- ◆ How to print a banner on a cut-sheet printer
- ◆ How to align labels and how to choose a starting place on the sheet of labels
- ◆ How to position envelopes for printing
- ◆ What to do if you're getting only a partial printout of a project

And best of all, you know everything you ever wanted to know about Print Shop Deluxe Ensemble II. You can create great things; we'll leave you now to do just that.

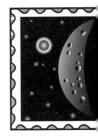

Appendices

Appendix

A

Installing Print Shop Deluxe Ensemble II

Installing Print Shop Deluxe Ensemble II is easy. The installation procedure outlined below lets you install the entire contents in just a few simple steps.

◆ Starting the Installation

1. Insert the CD into your CD-ROM drive (using a disc caddy if applicable).

2. Run the Setup program. If you are running Windows 3.1 from the Program Manager, choose Run under the File menu. If you are running Windows 95, click on the Start button and choose Run from the pop-up menu.

3. Type the following in the Command Line edit area: **D:\SETUP**
(where *D* is the designation of your CD-ROM drive). If you have
trouble installing from a CD-ROM, make sure you are typing the
correct letter when you are attempting to install.

4. Click on OK twice.

The Print Shop Deluxe Ensemble Setup program window will appear on
your screen, allowing you to choose between installing the Print Shop
Deluxe Ensemble *program* and/or installing the Print Shop Deluxe
Ensemble *fonts*.

◆ Program Installation

The Setup program will copy all the files needed to run the application
to your hard drive. You will be prompted to make installation decisions
such as whether or not to install the graphics libraries, ready-made projects, and additional fonts to your hard drive. A directory will be created
on your hard drive to store all program files and any projects you wish
to save. The application icons will be added to the Program Manager
(Windows 3.1) or Start menu (Windows 95).

1. Choose Program Installation.

2. You will be asked where you would like the Graphic Libraries and
Ready Made projects stored. You can choose to install them onto
your hard drive or keep them on CD.

If you choose to keep these files on the CD, then the Print Shop Deluxe
Ensemble CD must be loaded into the CD-ROM drive prior to launching.

3. By default, the Setup program will install all of the fonts that come
with the package. You will be asked whether or not you would like
to select only certain fonts to save disk space.

◆ If you choose Continue, skip ahead to step 4.

◆ If you choose Select Fonts, the Font Installation window will
appear, allowing you to choose the fonts you wish to install.

Click on the names of the fonts you wish to install. Clicking on an already highlighted font name will deselect it. If you wish to install all the fonts, click on the Select All button. The disk space requirements for the selected fonts will appear at the bottom of the window. When you are finished selecting the fonts, click on Continue.

4. The Setup Program will offer a default directory path and name to store the necessary files. If you want the files to be stored in a different directory, or on a different hard disk, modify the path as necessary.

5. After selecting a destination, click on Continue.

The installer will check to see that you have enough hard disk space to install the selected files.

The installer will also check to see if you have an older Windows version of a Print Shop Deluxe program on your hard drive. If the installer finds an older version, you will have the option of having the older version uninstalled. Your saved projects and any graphic library not included with the Print Shop Deluxe Ensemble will be moved to the new Projects and Libs directories.

6. The applications directory will be created if it doesn't already exist, and the necessary files will be copied to your hard drive. The selected fonts will be installed into your Windows System directory and the icons for the programs will be added to the Program Manager or Start menu. You will be returned to the Setup program window. Here, you can choose to install additional fonts or exit the Setup program.

◆ Starting the Program

Once the Print Shop Deluxe Ensemble has been installed, you will be returned to the Windows Program Manager (in Windows 3.1). The Setup program will have created a new program group called The Print Shop Deluxe Ensemble, which contains the Print Shop Deluxe Ensemble, the

Read Me First icon, and the Ensemble Graphics Exporter icon. Under Windows 95, you'll find your icons in the Start menu under Programs.

1. To start Print Shop, double-click on its icon in the Program Manager (Windows 3.1) or under Programs in the Start menu (Windows 95).

2. You will be prompted to personalize your program, and then the title screen for the program you have started will be displayed while the program is loading. When loading is finished, the Select a Project dialog will appear and you can start using the Print Shop Deluxe Ensemble II.

APPENDIX

B

A Compilation of Notes

Following is a compilation of the notes that appeared in this book. These are valuable tips for operating the program efficiently, and we thought they'd make a great reference library for you. The original location of each note is indicated by chapter number and heading. If you have any questions about a note, please refer to the chapter for further information.

◆ Chapter 1: Creating Your First Project

Starting a Project

Choosing an Orientation

All Greeting Card layouts work with one sheet of 8½" by 11" paper, folded to fit the specific card orientation. The Side Fold selection gives you four panels 5½" high by 4¼" wide, the Top Fold selection gives you four panels 4¼" high by 5½" wide, and the Top Fold Spread gives you a front and back panel 5½" wide by 4¼" high with the inside panel 5½" wide by 8½" high. (The actual printable area for each spread is somewhat smaller.)

Designing the Front of the Card

The first thing you'll be asked to design is the front of the greeting card. You'll design the inside and back of the greeting card after you reach the main project window.

Creating a Headline

Headline text sizes itself to fit the headline placeholder box. If you want a smaller or larger text type, resize the headline box, and the text will automatically resize to fit the new box.

Editing Text

The Preview button becomes the Edit button when you are in preview mode. If you want to change the text, click on Edit and the text box changes back to normal so you can change or add to the text (the button changes back to Preview at the same time).

Moving Objects

It is important to remember that you must select the object or text with the Pointer tool before you can do anything to it. Menus and tool options will be offered based on what you've selected to edit. If you've selected a graphic, graphic options will be available. If you've selected text, text options will be offered.

Adding a Graphic

You can pull down the names of more graphics libraries if you cannot find what you're looking for in this one. Print Shop Deluxe Ensemble II has some 4500 graphics available for your projects. We'll talk more about graphics and graphics libraries in Part II, "Managing Graphics."

◆ Chapter 2: Discovering Tools

Starting the Project

Ready-made projects are complete and can be printed out as is; however, you can personalize them by adding or deleting objects, changing the backdrop, altering the layout, changing the page color, or anything else.

Moving and Resizing Objects

Moving a Single Object

All objects have four corners, regardless of what is inside the object area. The bucket, for example, appears to be just a bucket, but when you select it, you can see it is in a square box. The same would be true no matter what size and shape the graphics or text inside a box. The box always has four corners and four handles.

Resizing Graphics

When resizing an object, you select a handle to pull or push the object to its new size. The opposite handle becomes an anchor for the object and does not move from its original position as you resize. If, for example, you pull on the handle in the upper-right corner, all corners of the object except the lower-left one move.

Aspect Ratio is the relationship between the width and the height of an object. For instance, the aspect ratio of the bucket in our sign appears to be 1:1, which means it is a square, just as wide as it is tall. We could resize it, making it larger but keeping it a square. Or we could reshape it, changing the aspect ratio by stretching it or squeezing it into another shape, say a rectangle.

Resizing Headline or Text Blocks

You can resize two or more objects simultaneously in exactly the same way that you would resize one by linking the items together. You link the objects together by selecting them all using the Pointer tool and your

Shift key. If one of the objects in the linked objects is a graphic, you follow the procedure for resizing graphics. If all the objects in the linked objects are text or headline blocks, use the process for resizing text or headline blocks.

Moving Around in the Document

The Hand tool is not available when a project fits inside the viewing window, since no part of the project is hidden from view.

You can also move around a project that is larger than the viewing window by using the scroll bars at the right and bottom edges of the window. Click on the button located inside the scroll bar and drag the button to move through the project. You'll notice that when you use the Hand tool, the scroll bars move as you move around.

Deleting Objects

If you wish to undelete the last deletion, click on the Undo tool, the U-shaped arrow on the toolbar. Remember, only the last thing you deleted can be restored. See "Undoing or Redoing Your Last Action" later in the chapter for more on the Undo tool.

Framing Objects

Note that the frames you've just added are black. This is the default color for frames. You can change this color, choosing from a selection of different colors offered on the palette in the Color Selector. We'll talk about that in "Coloring and Shading an Area" later in this chapter.

Undoing or Redoing Your Last Action
Redoing Your Last Action

If you've performed any actions after clicking the Undo tool, the tool will not act as a Redo tool; instead, clicking it will undo the most recent change.

Coloring and Shading an Area

You cannot change colors for a multicolored object, but you can change the saturation of these colors in increments of 10%. The lower the percentage, the lighter the color.

In some cases, the graphic may cover the entire object area. When this happens, you cannot color behind the object because there is no area behind the object that you can see.

◆ Chapter 3: Mastering Menus

Some commands can also be accessed using keyboard shortcuts. Where applicable, these shortcuts are noted next to the corresponding menu commands. For example, in the File menu you can see that the keyboard shortcut for the Open command is Ctrl+O. The next time you want to open a project, you can just press Ctrl+O instead of selecting File ➤ Open.

Using the Edit Menu

You must select an object before you can use most of the Edit commands. If no object is selected, the only edit option available is Select All.

Selecting All

You can use the Select All command to identify all the objects in a project. This is particularly useful when you're working with a ready-made project and are not quite sure, for example, where one text block ends and another begins or whether an image is one large graphic or a combination of several graphics.

Using the Object Menu

Putting Objects in Order

You cannot place objects behind the backdrop; it will always be the bottom layer of the project. And you cannot place objects in front of a border;

it will always be the top layer. (If you really want to place objects in front of a border, there's a way around this: make a mini-border and stretch it to fit the page. You *can* place objects in front of a mini-border.)

Scaling an Object

Remember that scaling a text box does not change the size of the type. If the box gets too small for the type size or content, type will be hidden outside the box.

Using the Project Menu

Changing the Backdrop

When you change a backdrop, all the layout elements remain the same and maintain the same position they had with the previous backdrop.

If you've experimented with several backdrops and you want to go back to having no backdrop at all, you won't be able to use the Undo command, since that only undoes your most recent action. But you can still return to a blank background by scrolling to the top of the list of graphics and selecting Blank Page.

Changing the Banner Length

Changing the banner length stretches the backdrop and any headlines but does not stretch any graphics on the banner. All these stay in essentially the same position as they were before the stretch. You'll need to grab handles and manually stretch graphics to fill the new space.

◆ Chapter 4: Getting Help

Using the Main Help Screen

Help screens have three different linked elements—pop-up boxes, jumps, and notes. Whenever you move your cursor over one of these links, the cursor will change to a hand, indicating a link command. Green text is linked to a pop-up box that offers additional information about the current subject. Underlined green text is linked to a jump, which takes you directly to another Help screen. A note icon offers additional information on the current topic or a related topic when you click on it.

Using Links

The left arrow button moves you between screens but does not necessarily return you to the last screen, since there are topics embedded in screens. If you want to go to a previous screen, use Go Back.

Using the Help Menu Bar
Using the Edit Menu

To delete a bookmark, you can click on Edit ➤ Place a Bookmark, select the bookmark you want to delete, and click on Delete.

◆ Chapter 5: Understanding Print Shop Projects

Project-Specific Design Elements
Designing Greeting Cards

Greeting cards and postcards (discussed under "Designing Stationery" later in the chapter) are the only multipage projects in Print Shop. To move from page to page in these projects, you use the Navigation tool. (See Chapter 1 for more information about the Navigation tool.)

Remember, you're filling a wide space in the side-fold spread card, so tall backdrops will be stretched to fit.

◆ Chapter 6: Working with Graphics Libraries

Types of Graphics

To reach a Graphics Browser that offers all graphic shapes, select Object ➤ Add. The first item listed is Graphics. Click on this instead of one of the shapes offered and you go immediately to a Graphics Browser where you can search all shapes and all libraries. Selecting All Shapes and All Libraries as a search criterion is a quick way to search every graphic available at the same time.

Navigating the Graphics Browser

Starting a Project

In all the projects except Labels and Calendars, you can quickly reach the main project window from the Orientation screen by holding down the Ctrl key while clicking on the orientation of your project. This action bypasses the backdrop and layout options.

Broadening the Search Options

You can change the type of graphic in the Graphics Browser window. While you started with a square graphic in this search, you could switch to a column graphic, row graphic, or mini-backdrop by simply selecting one of these from the Graphic Shape drop-down list. The placeholder in the project will change its shape to accommodate the new graphic choice.

Searching by Multiple Keywords

When a search is in progress, the Search button changes to a Stop button. If you want to stop the search, click on it.

Searching with Project Text

When you add project text, any keywords you already have in the keywords box will be replaced by the project text.

Merging Graphics Libraries

You cannot modify the original Print Shop libraries. The program will not allow you to delete graphics from the original libraries, so don't worry about deleting graphics by mistake. However, once you've merged original libraries into a new custom library, you can delete, rename, or add to the copied graphics.

Preparing to Merge Libraries

You can also search for other graphics libraries by changing your directory or drive on the left side of the Merge Libraries dialog box. However, any graphics you merge must be Print Shop graphics, meaning libraries with file names ending in .psg, .cbr, .pbr, .pcg, .prg, .prl, .pse, and .psi.

Modifying Graphics Libraries

Modifying a Library

When you delete a graphic, there is no prompt asking you if you're sure you want to delete it. Once you have hit the Delete key, the graphic is gone and you cannot undo the deletion. But because the custom library was created by merging two Print Shop libraries, the graphic still exists intact in one of the two Print Shop libraries you merged. Therefore, you could retrieve the graphic from its original file. If the deleted graphic is one you created, however, it's gone for good, unless you stored it in another library as well.

◆ Chapter 7: Creating Special Graphics

Customizing Smart Graphics

You can also reach smart graphics from the main project window by selecting Extras from the main menu, clicking on Smart Graphics, and choosing from the drop-down list offering Initial Caps, Numbers, Timepieces, and Borders. If you select Initial Caps, for instance, the Create an Initial Cap dialog box will pop up.

Designing an Initial Cap

The design elements offered in the Create an Initial Cap dialog box are not limited to upper- and lowercase letters. You can type anything into the Letter box, including numbers or symbols. You can also design number graphics by choosing Smart Graphics ➤ Numbers, but special symbol graphics can only be designed in the Initial Cap area.

If you save an initial cap without adding it to the project (by clicking on the Save button instead of the Add to Project button), you can retrieve it by adding a square graphic and double-clicking on its placeholder to reach the Graphics Browser. Change the library to your library name (in this case Letter), find the graphic (dance1), and insert it into the project.

Selecting a Timepiece

You can select No Graphic in the Select a Timepiece dialog box, but it's not a real option. If you select No Graphic and click OK, you are sent back to the Smart Graphics menu or to the main project window, depending on which method you used to get here. Selecting No Graphic is the same thing as clicking on Cancel.

There is no a.m. or p.m. indication on either analog or digital clocks. If you use a 24-hour clock and enter 19:00 as the time, it will be displayed as 7:00.

Designing a Seal

Adding Text

You can change the color of monochrome graphics, text, and bullets in the main project window also: select the seal, click on the Item Selector, and choose Object, then use the Color Selector to change the color. To change the color behind the seal, select Behind Object from the Item Selector and then select a color.

◆ Chapter 8: Importing Images

Importing Graphics

Different programs save graphics as different file types. A graphic from Microsoft Word's Clipart directory, for example, is saved as a Windows Metafile (WMF), while a graphic from Broderbund's Kid Pix for Windows is a bitmap file (BMP).

Looking at Available Files

BMP files can be cropped before they are imported into the project. Cropping is available only for BMP files, not for WMF, TIFF, or EPS files. Refer to the "Cropping Photos" section later in this chapter for more on using this cropping option.

Importing a Graphic

Imported color graphics will always display in color if you have a color monitor. Even if you are working in grayscale, imported color graphics will be displayed in color. Changing the color preference in the main project window does not affect the way imported color graphics are displayed.

◆ Chapter 9: Exporting Graphics

Choosing a Graphic

If you need some help finding the right graphic for a particular project, use the advanced Search options in the Graphics Browser to pinpoint the graphic(s) you want. You'll need to do this before you select the Graphics Exporter. The Graphics Browser is discussed in more detail in Chapter 1.

Exporting a Graphic

Designating a File Type

The Graphics Exporter's EPS format saves EPS files without preview. This means that when you import these EPS files into a project outside Print Shop, you will not see a preview of the graphic. Rather, you see only a box representing the graphic's location. You can resize and move this box but you will not see the actual graphic until you print the project. Also, keep in mind that it takes a PostScript printer to print an EPS file. If you don't have a PostScript printer, do not export graphics as EPS files.

If you have selected multiple graphics for export, you cannot change any of their names. They will all be exported under the names given to them in Print Shop. You can change their names in Windows File Manager or Windows Explorer outside Print Shop after they have been exported, if you like.

Choosing a Destination

Remember that when you export graphics, only copies of the original files are exported. The Print Shop files remain intact and the original libraries are not altered in any way.

Exporting a Library
Printing a Catalog

If you are printing more than one copy of a library, you may want to collate the printed pages. To do this, check the Collate Copies box in the lower-right corner of the Print dialog box; the computer will print all of the pages of one copy before printing the next copy. If Collate Copies is not selected, the printer will print all of the copies of page one, followed by all copies of page two, and so on, and you will have to sort them manually.

◆ Chapter 10: Working with Text and Headlines

Editing Text Blocks
Choosing Text Attributes

When text is highlighted, any numeric or alphabetic key you hit erases all the highlighted text. This is especially important to remember when you first enter the Edit Text dialog box because all existing text is highlighted. If you erase text accidentally, click on Cancel to exit the Edit Text dialog box. This cancels anything you did and restores the text. You can then reopen the dialog box and begin editing again.

You cannot type in the preview area when you are in preview mode. When you are in preview mode, the Preview button changes to an Edit button. Click on the Edit button to return to the text box where you can type any changes to the text.

The text preview box is not the same size as the actual text block on the sign. The preview area does, however, display the text as it will appear in the text block based on the current size, font, and style. You can, of course, change the size of the text block when you return to the main project window if you need to make room for more text.

There are two other important options in the Edit Text dialog box: List Merge and Quotes and Verses, but don't worry about either of these just now. The list merge commands are covered extensively in Chapter 10, "Creating and Merging Lists," and we'll cover Quotes and Verses later in this chapter.

Working with Headlines

You cannot change the size of the type in a headline. The type expands or contracts to fill the headline box. If you want smaller type, make the headline box smaller. If you want larger type, make the box larger. See "Resizing Headline or Text Blocks" in Chapter 2 for instructions.

Customizing Headline Text

Like the Edit Text dialog box, the Headline dialog box has a List Merge button. We'll cover the list merge options in Chapter 11, "Creating and Merging Lists."

Working with Title Blocks

Choosing Type Specs for Title Blocks

Neither section of the Title Block dialog box offers specific text size options. As you remember, a headline will size to fit its box, and the secondary line is sized in relation to the headline.

Adding a Word Balloon

The tail position of a word balloon varies depending on its original design in the Select a Balloon Type dialog box. For example, if the tail starts in the center position in this dialog box, the tail will shift only slightly left and right. On the other hand, if the tail points far left in the dialog box, it will point far right when you select Right as the tail position and will be centered when you select Center.

The Edit Word Balloon Text dialog box includes a List Merge button and a Quotes and Verses button, making both of these options available to insert into your word balloon. See Chapter 11 for information about merging lists, and see "Exploring Quotes and Verses" later in this chapter for information about those elements.

Exploring Quotes and Verses

If you wanted to add a quote or verse to a text block, you would double-click on the text block to open the Edit Text dialog box, and then click on the Quotes and Verses button there. Quotes and Verses are not available from any other source in PSD Ensemble II.

◆ Chapter 11: Creating and Merging Lists

Creating Lists

Making an Address List

Use Tab to move down the dialog box from one text box to the next. Use Shift+Tab to move up through the boxes. You can also use your mouse to move from box to box.

If you are creating an address list of company names rather than individuals, you can type the name of the company in the Last Name line and nothing in the First Name line, or you can split the company name to fill both the First Name and Last Name lines. If you split the name, remember that the list will be arranged alphabetically based on what is entered in the Last Name line.

Every address list or custom list file can include up to 200 entries, and you can create an unlimited number of address or custom lists.

If you want to create an address or custom list that includes many entries from another list, open the existing list file, as noted above, and use the Save As command from the File menu to save it under a different name. Then open the second file and customize it to your liking.

Merging Lists

Choosing a List to Merge

If you prefer, you can wait until after you have selected your merge fields (see the next section) to select the file to merge into.

Selecting Merge Fields

You can choose a font, type size, style, and color for a merge field in the Edit Text dialog box just as you would for any other text.

Do not be concerned if you do not want the first person on the list to get this envelope. You will have the opportunity to select exactly who on this address list gets the mailing when you actually print the project.

Printing a List

See "Printing a Name List" in Chapter 12 for information on dealing with problems you might encounter when you print using a list merge.

◆ Chapter 12: Printing Made Easy

Printing Specific Projects

Printing Envelopes

An aerogram is a type of envelope used mainly for international letters. To create an aerogram, select Aerogram to print the envelope's address in the center of a regular sheet of paper. Turn the page over, feed it back into the printer, and print the message on the opposite side. Then fold the page in thirds so that the address side is out. Put a stamp on it and mail it.

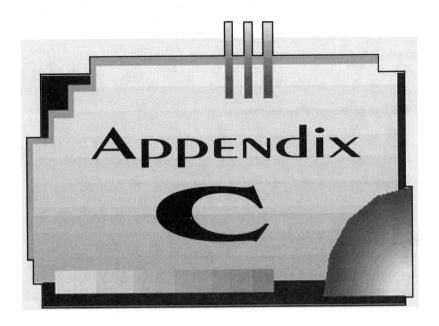

Specialized Paper Sources

Projects look great printed on specialty paper. Here are our favorite paper companies. Give them a call for a catalog.

Avery®

A complete line of laser labels and card products, ink jet labels, index products, and Communique specialty papers.

Phone	800-252-8379	Mon–Fri 8 a.m.– 4 p.m. PST
Fax	800-862-8379	7 days a week, 24 hours a day

Beaver Prints™

Innovative laser papers including preprinted photography! Great prices. Unique products, brochures, letterhead, envelopes, specialty products.

Hundreds of designs and formats!

Phone	800-923-2837	Mon–Fri 8 a.m.– 9 p.m. EST
		Sat 9 a.m.–12:30 p.m. EST
Fax	800-232-8374	7 days a week, 24 hours a day

Idea Art

Over a thousand choices of high-quality, environmentally friendly designs for brochures, flyers, newsletters, invitations, and more. All papers are recycled and printed with natural soy inks.

| Phone | 800-433-2278 | Mon–Fri 7:30 a.m.–6 p.m. CST |
| Fax | 800-435-2278 | 7 days a week, 24 hours a day |

Paper Access

Over 500 unique preprinted and unprinted papers in a full range of items and sizes.

Phone	800-727-3701	Mon–Fri 9 a.m.–7 p.m. EST
		Sat 11 a.m.–6 p.m. EST
Fax	212-924-7318	7 days a week, 24 hours a day

Paper Direct®

Thousands of specialty preprinted and unprinted papers, envelopes, labels, and presentation products.

Phone	800-272-7377	Mon–Fri 8 a.m.–9 p.m. EST
		Sat 10 a.m.–4 p.m. EST
Fax	201-271-9601	7 days a week, 24 hours a day

Queblo®

Elegant embossed and foil-stamped papers; designs for brochures, newsletters, and business cards; full-color labels; and much more. Money-back guarantee and fast delivery.

Phone	800-523-9080	Mon–Fri 7:30 a.m.–7:30 p.m. EST
Fax	800-554-8779	7 days a week, 24 hours a day

Index

Note to the Reader: **Boldface** numbers indicate pages where you will find the principal discussion of a topic or the definition of a term. *Italic* numbers indicate pages where topics are illustrated in figures.

A

Add command, 70. *See also* adding objects

adding
graphics, 18–21, 25. *See also* New object tool
headlines, **193–199**
objects, **42–46**
text, 15–16, 24, **187–212**. *See also* New object tool
to seals, 162–163
to signature blocks, 204–206
word balloons, 206–209

Address List dialog box, 214–218, *215*
maximum number of characters per text box, 215–216

address lists, **213–218**, *215*
maximum number of entries, 217

aerograms, 235

aligning objects, 79–80

alignment buttons, 192–193, *192–193*

Annotate dialog box, 96, *96*

aspect ratio, **35–37**

attributes
headline text, **195–196**

for signature lines, 202–203
text, 189–191
autographs, inserting, 204

B

backdrop libraries, 126–127

backdrops
changing, 80–81
lightening, 106
previewing, 10
searching, 8–9, 104
selecting, 7, 21–22, 104

Backdrops Browser, 7–10, *8, 9, 103*, 104, *105*

Banner dialog box, *111*, 111–112

banner length, changing, 82–84

Banner Length dialog box, 82, *82*

Banner Orientation dialog box, 104, *104*

Banner Size option, 112

banners
adding text to, 111
designing, **61–88, 110–112**
horizontal, 112
vertical, 112

BMP (Windows Bitmaps), 166–169

bold type, 13, 16

Bookmark Define dialog box, 97, *97*

bookmarks
    creating, 110
    deleting, 97

border arrangement options
    Alternating Rails, *156*
    changing the arrangement, 155
    Corners and Rails, *156*
    Rails with Centerpieces, *157*
    Single Piece Repeating, *155*

Border Type dialog box, 154, *154*

borders
    adding to a project, 160
    customizing, *154*, 154–160, *155*
    saving, 159

bumper stickers, creating, 108–110, *110*

C

Calendar Day dialog box, 117, *117*, 118

Calendar options, *118*, 118–119

calendar type, *116*, 116–117

calendars, designing, **116–119**
    adding graphics, 117–118
    adding text, 117
    daily, 117

cancel in Edit Text dialog box, 190

category keywords
    in Backdrops Browser, 9, *9*
    in Graphics Browser, 20, 130
    in Quotes and Verses Browser dialog box, 210, *210*

centering text, 16

certificates, designing, **112–114, 147–149**

Change Shape button in Edit Word Balloon Text dialog box, 207

Clipboard, 66–67

ClipPix file, 169–170

collating copies when printing, 182

Color box
    for headline text, 199
    for initial cap, 147

color changing of the type, 17

coloring an area, 51–53

Coloring Book option, 63

Copy command, **67**

covering up part of an object, 121–122

Create a Border dialog box, *155*, 155–158, *156*, *158*

Create a Number dialog box, 150–151, *151*

Create an Initial Cap dialog box, *145*, 145–146, 149

creating lists, 214–220, *215*, *219*
    maximum number of entries, 217

Crop Marks option, 115

cropping photos, 168, 172–173

Custom Effect dialog box, *14*, 14–15, 73, *73*, *198*, 198–199

custom libraries, creating, **134–141**

Custom Library dialog box, 135, *135*

Custom List dialog box, 214, 218–220, *219*

custom lists, 213–214, **218–220**, *219*
   maximum number of entries, 217
customized seals, saving, 163–164
customizing
   headline text, **197–199**, *198*
   libraries, 87
   text, 14–15
Cut command, **66–67**

D

Daily Calendar Options dialog box, 118, *118*
Decorative Numbers library, 152
default graphics library. *See* PSD (Print Shop Deluxe) Backdrops
Delete command, **68**
Delete tool, **47**
deleting objects, 47, 68
dialog box. *See individual entries*
drop shadow
   for headline text, 199
   for initial cap, 147, *147*
Duplicate command, **68–69**

E

Edit Hour dialog box, 117–118, *118*
Edit menu, **65–70**
   from Help screen, 96
Edit Signature Block dialog box, 202–203, *203*
   Justification box, 203
Edit Text dialog box, 16, *16*, 72, *72*, *189*

Edit Word Balloon Text dialog box, 207, *207*
   Change Shape button, 207
   List Merge button, 209
   Quotes and Verses button, 209
editing
   graphics, 71
   headlines, 73–74
   objects, **70–74**
   text, **15–17**, 71–72, **187–193**
   text blocks, 188–193
envelopes, 222–227
EPS (Encapsulated Postscript Files), 166–169
exiting Print Shop Deluxe Ensemble II, 65
exporting
   graphics, 87. *See also* Graphics Exporter
   lists, 228–229
Extra Features dialog box, 135, *135*
Extras menu, 86–87
extras, creating, **144–160**. *See also* Select a Project dialog box

F

File menu, **56–65**
   from Help screen, 95
   Preferences dialog box, *61*, 61–62
file types, 136, 166–169
Flip command. *See* Flip tool
Flip tool, **48**
flipping objects, **48**
font, changing, 13
frame, adding color to, 53

Frame command. *See* Frame tool
Frame tool, **48–49**, 53
framing
    objects, **48**, *49*
    the text box, 25–26

G

gift wrapping paper, creating, 110
Graphic Data option in Save
    command, 59
Graphic Library box, 8
graphics, resizing, 35–36, 38
Graphics Browser, *19*, 19–20, 25,
    127–134, *128, 131, 132*, 177
    search options, 20, 177
    searching
        by category, 130
        by keywords, 130
        by multiple keywords,
          130–133
Graphics Exporter, **175–183**
    assigning a name, 179
    choosing a destination, 180
    choosing a graphic, 176–178
    collating pages when printing,
      182
    designating a file type,
      178–179
    dialog box, 176–177, *177*
    exiting, 183
    exporting
        a graphic, 178–180, *179*
        a library, 180–181
        all graphics, 177–178
    opening, 176
    printing
        a catalog, 181–182

        to a file, 182
    graphics libraries, 181–182
Graphics Exporter dialog box,
    176–177, *177*
graphics libraries, 8, 126–127
    merging, **134–141**
    working with, **125–141**
graphics types, 126–127
    backdrops, 126–127
    graphics, 126–127
    layouts, 126
graphics
    adding. *See* adding graphics
    changing
        shape of, 36
        type of, 129
    exporting, 87. *See also* Graphics
      Exporter
    importing, **165–169**, *167*
        allowable file types, 166–169
    rotating. *See* rotating graphics
greeting cards, creating, **4–27**,
    107–108
    designing
        the back, 24–27
        the front, 7–21
        the inside, 21–24
    orientation, *6*, 6–7
    side fold, 6–7
    side fold spread, 6–7
    top fold, 6–7
    top fold spread, 6–7

H

Hand tool, **40–41**, 46
handles, 18, 33, 34, 35
headline blocks, resizing, 36–38

Headline dialog box, 13, *13*, 73,
    73, 111, **193–197**, *194*, 199
  justify, 196
  shape option, 196
headline text
  attributes, **195–196**
  customizing, 14, **197–199**, *198*
  editing, 73–74
  resizing, 13
  shadow option, 199
  shape box, 199
headlines, adding, **193–199**
Help in dialog boxes, 99
Help, getting, 88, **89–100**, *90*
  searching, 93–95
  using Help chapters, 92
  using keyboard shortcuts,
    92–93
  using links, 91
Help library, 98–99. *See also* Help,
    getting
Help menu bar, **95–100**
  Edit menu, 96
    Annotate dialog box, 96, *96*
    Bookmark Define dialog
      box, 97, *97*
  File menu, 95
  Help menu, 98
  Topics menu, 98
Help screen, main, *90*

I

Import Graphic dialog box, 167,
    167, 171
importable files, saving projects
    as, 169

importing
  graphics, **165–169**, *167*
    allowable file types, 166–169
  lists, 228
  photos, **169–173**
Include Preview option in Save
    command, 59
initial cap, designing, **145–150**
inserting autographs, 204
installing Print Shop Deluxe
    Ensemble II, **241–244**
italics, 13

J

Justification box in Edit Signature
    Block dialog box, 203
justify in Headline dialog box,
    196

K

keyboard shortcuts, **56**
  in Help system, 92–93
keywords, searching by in
    Graphics Browser, 130–133

L

labels, designing, **119–121**
  Select a Label Type dialog box,
    121, *121*
  Starting Place dialog box, 120,
    120
layout libraries, 126
layouts
  changing, 81–82
  selecting, 11, *11*, 22, 105–106,
    106
Lighten Backdrop box, 106

List Merge button in Edit Word
    Balloon Text dialog box, 209
lists
    accessing, 87
    address, **213–218**, *215*
    creating, 214–220, *215, 219*
    custom, 213–214, **218–220**,
        219
    exporting, 228–229
    importing, 228
    maximum number of entries,
        217
    merging, 221–225
    modifying, 220–221
    printing, 226–227
locking objects, **78–79**, 111

M

main menu, **55–56**
main project window, 31, 32, *32*,
    129
Match All Keywords option, 131,
    132
Match Any Keywords option,
    130–131, 134
menus, **55–100**
merge fields, selecting, 224–225
Merge Libraries dialog box, 136,
    136
merging
    graphics libraries, **134–141**
    lists, 221–225
mirroring options in Create a
    Border dialog box, 157
Modify Library dialog box,
    138–140, *139*

modifying
    graphics libraries, **138–140**
    lists, 220–221
Month Thumbnails, 119, *119*
Monthly Calendar Options dialog
    box, 119
moving objects, 18, 33–35

N

Name Graphic Library dialog
    box, 137, *137*
Name List option, 114
naming Smart Graphics, 154
Navigation tool, **21**
New object tool, 42–46
note compilation, 245–260
numbers, designing, **150–152**

O

Object menu, **70–80**
Open a List File dialog box, 224,
    226
opening files, **57–58**, *58*
Order command, 75–76
orientation, 103–104

P

Page Blend option, 53, **84–85**
paper sources, **261–263**
Paste command, **67–68**
photos
    cropping, 168, **172–173**
    importing, **169–173**
    memory requirements for,
        171–172
    resizing, 173
    resolutions of, 171
    viewing from CD, 170

pixelize, 169
placeholders, **12–17**, 20, 23,
   42–43, **42–46**
  graphics, 12, 20
  headline, 12–13, 23
  text, 12, 23
Pointer tool, **18**, 33–35
postcard layout, U.S. Postal
   Service approved, 116
postcards, 222
  designing, **115–116**
PostScript fonts, 237
Preferences dialog box, *61*, 61–62
preview, 64–65
previewing
  backdrops, 10
  layouts, 23
  text, 16
Print dialog box, 63, *63*, 115,
   115, 120, *120*, *181*, 182, 226,
   226
Print Shop Deluxe Ensemble II
   program installation, 241–244
Print Shop toolbar, 32–33, *33*
printing, **63–64**, 181–182
  a catalog, 181–182
  collating copies, 182
  to a file, 182
  a graphics library, 181–182
  lists, 226–227
  with PostScript fonts, 237
  projects, **231–238**
    aerograms, 235
    banners, 232–233
    business cards, 234–235
    envelopes, 235–236
    labels, 233–234

    labels, Starting Place dialog
      box for, 234, *234*
    name lists, 233
  on supported printers, 231–232
  troubleshooting problems,
    236–237
  with TrueType fonts, 237
Project menu, **80–86**
project window, 31, 32, *32*, 129
PSD (Print Shop Deluxe)
   Backdrops, 104
PSD (Print Shop Deluxe) Squares
   library, 19

Q

Quotes and Verses Browser,
   209–210, *210*
Quotes and Verses Browser dialog
   box, **209–210**, *210*
Quotes and Verses button in Edit
   Word Balloon Text dialog
   box, 209
quotes, adding, **209–211**, *210*

R

Ready-made, 4–5, 30, 31,
   102–103
Red Sundays, 119
Redo tool, **50**
redoing your last action, 50
Rename Graphic dialog box, 140,
   140
resizing
  graphics, 35–36, 38
  headline or text blocks, 36–38
  objects, 35–36, 38
  photos, 173

Return Address dialog box, 223, *223*

Revert to Saved command, **61**

Rotate command, 77–78

Rotate dialog box, 78, *78*

Rotate envelope option, 62

Rotate tool, **38–39**

rotating graphics, **38–39**

S

Save Graphic in Library dialog box, 148, *148*

Save a List File dialog box, 217, *217*, 220

saving
  coordinated projects, 114–115
  a custom border, 159
  customized seals, 163–164
  files, **58–60**, *59*
    file types, 59
    Graphic Data option, 59
    Include Preview option, 59
  Print Shop projects as importable files, 169
  seals, 163–164
  Smart Graphics, 154

saving as, 60

Scale command, 76–77

Scale dialog box, 77, *77*

Scroll bar, **41**

Seal dialog box, 160–161, *161*

seals
  adding text to, 162–163
  changing color behind, 163
  coordinated graphics for, 162

  designing, 113, *161, 162*, **162–164**
  saving, 163–164

Search dialog box, *93*, 93–95

Search Options dialog box, 94, *94*

search options
  in Backdrops Browser, 8–9
  in Graphics Browser, 20, **127–134**, 177
  in Quotes and Verses Browser dialog box, 210–211

Search Preferences dialog box, 131

Search Results dialog box, 94, *94*

search, stopping, 133

searching with project text, 133–134

Select a Label Type dialog box, 121, *121*

Select a Layout dialog box, 11, *11*, 105–106, *106*

Select a Path dialog box, 4–5, *5*

Select a Project dialog box, 4–5, *5*

Select a Ready Made sign window, *31*

Select a Seal Center dialog box, 161, *161*

Select a Seal Edge dialog box, 162, *162*

Select a Timepiece dialog box, 152–153, *153*
  No Graphic selection, 153

Select All command, **69–70**

Select List Entries dialog box, 227, *227*

shading an area, 51–53

Shadow command, 74–75
Shadow effect for initial cap, 147, *147*
shadow option for headline text, 199
shadow type, 16
Shape box, 73
    for headline text, 199
shape option in Headline dialog box, 196
Shrink printout option, 62
sign theme window, *30*
signature block, 113, **201–206**
    adding text to, 204
    selecting type, 202
signature lines, text attributes for, 202–203
Signature Type dialog box, 202, *202*
signs and posters, designing, 30–54, **108–110**
silhouette option
    for headline text, 199
    for initial cap, 147, *147*, 150
Size option for banner, 112
Skip optional dialogs option, 62
Smart Graphics, 87
    customizing, **144–160**
    dialog box, *144*, 144–145
    naming, 154
    saving, 154
Start From Scratch, 4–5, 30, 103–106
Starting Place dialog box, 120, *120, 121*, 234, *234*
starting Print Shop Deluxe Ensemble II, 243–244

stationery, designing, **114–116**
suffix for numbers, 151
summary of steps, 245–260

T

tail position of word balloon, 207
text, adding, **187–212**
text attributes, 189–191
    for signature lines, 202–203
text bar, *191*, 191–193
    alignment buttons, 192–193, *192–193*
text blocks
    editing, 188–193
    resizing, 36–38
text formats, *188*, **188–212**
    headlines, 193–199
    quotes and verses, 209–211
    signature blocks, 201–206
    text blocks, 188–193
    title blocks, 200
    word balloons, 206–209
Thumbnails. *See* Month Thumbnails
TIFF (Tagged Image Files), 166–169
timepieces
    selecting, **152–154**, *153*
    selecting No Graphic, 153
Title Block dialog box, 200–201, *201*
title blocks, 200
toolbar, **32–33**, *33*
tools, **29–54**
troubleshooting print problems, 236–237
TrueType fonts, 237

types of graphics, 126–127
   backdrops, 126–127
   graphics, 126–127
   layouts, 126

U

U.S. Postal Service approved postcard layout, 116
undelete, **47–48**, **50**
Undo tool, 47–48, 50
undoing your last action, 47–48,
   50, 65–66
unlocking objects, 78–79

V

verses, adding, **209–211**, *210*
View menu, 86. *See also*
   Zoom tool

W

watermarked paper, creating, 113,
   113
Watermarked Text dialog box,
   113, *113*
WMF (Windows Metafiles),
   166–169
Word Balloon Type dialog box,
   206, 206–207
word balloon
   adding, 206–209
   tail position, 207

Y

Yearly Calendar Options dialog
   box, 119

Z

Zoom tool, **40–41**, 46

FOR EVERY COMPUTER QUESTION,
THERE IS A SYBEX BOOK THAT HAS THE ANSWER

Each computer user learns in a different way. Some need thorough, methodical explanations, while others are too busy for details. At Sybex we bring nearly 20 years of experience to developing the book that's right for you. Whatever your needs, we can help you get the most from your software and hardware, at a pace that's comfortable for you.

We start beginners out right. You will learn by seeing and doing with our **Quick & Easy** series: friendly, colorful guidebooks with screen-by-screen illustrations. For hardware novices, the **Your First** series offers valuable purchasing advice and installation support.

Often recognized for excellence in national book reviews, our **Mastering** titles are designed for the intermediate to advanced user, without leaving the beginner behind. A **Mastering** book provides the most detailed reference available. Add our pocket-sized **Instant Reference** titles for a complete guidance system. Programmers will find that the new **Developer's Handbook** series provides a more advanced perspective on developing innovative and original code.

With the breathtaking advances common in computing today comes an ever increasing demand to remain technologically up-to-date. In many of our books, we provide the added value of software, on disks or CDs. Sybex remains your source for information on software development, operating systems, networking, and every kind of desktop application. We even have books for kids. Sybex can help smooth your travels on the **Internet** and provide **Strategies and Secrets** to your favorite computer games.

As you read this book, take note of its quality. Sybex publishes books written by experts—authors chosen for their extensive topical knowledge. In fact, many are professionals working in the computer software field. In addition, each manuscript is thoroughly reviewed by our technical, editorial, and production personnel for accuracy and ease-of-use before you ever see it—our guarantee that you'll buy a quality Sybex book every time.

To manage your hardware headaches and optimize your software potential, ask for a Sybex book.

FOR MORE INFORMATION, PLEASE CONTACT:

Sybex Inc.
2021 Challenger Drive
Alameda, CA 94501
Tel: (510) 523-8233 • (800) 227-2346
Fax: (510) 523-2373

SYBEX

Sybex is committed to using natural resources wisely to preserve and improve our environment. As a leader in the computer books publishing industry, we are aware that over 40% of America's solid waste is paper. This is why we have been printing our books on recycled paper since 1982.

This year our use of recycled paper will result in the saving of more than 153,000 trees. We will lower air pollution effluents by 54,000 pounds, save 6,300,000 gallons of water, and reduce landfill by 27,000 cubic yards.

In choosing a Sybex book you are not only making a choice for the best in skills and information, you are also choosing to enhance the quality of life for all of us.

GET A FREE CATALOG JUST FOR EXPRESSING YOUR OPINION.

Help us improve our books and get a *FREE* full-color catalog in the bargain. Please complete this form, pull out this page and send it in today. The address is on the reverse side.

Name _____   Company _____

Address _____   City _____ State ____ Zip _____

Phone (___) _____

1. How would you rate the overall quality of this book?

- ❑ Excellent
- ❑ Very Good
- ❑ Good
- ❑ Fair
- ❑ Below Average
- ❑ Poor

2. What were the things you liked most about the book? (Check all that apply)

- ❑ Pace
- ❑ Format
- ❑ Writing Style
- ❑ Examples
- ❑ Table of Contents
- ❑ Index
- ❑ Price
- ❑ Illustrations
- ❑ Type Style
- ❑ Cover
- ❑ Depth of Coverage
- ❑ Fast Track Notes

3. What were the things you liked *least* about the book? (Check all that apply)

- ❑ Pace
- ❑ Format
- ❑ Writing Style
- ❑ Examples
- ❑ Table of Contents
- ❑ Index
- ❑ Price
- ❑ Illustrations
- ❑ Type Style
- ❑ Cover
- ❑ Depth of Coverage
- ❑ Fast Track Notes

4. Where did you buy this book?

- ❑ Bookstore chain
- ❑ Small independent bookstore
- ❑ Computer store
- ❑ Wholesale club
- ❑ College bookstore
- ❑ Technical bookstore
- ❑ Other _____

5. How did you decide to buy this particular book?

- ❑ Recommended by friend
- ❑ Recommended by store personnel
- ❑ Author's reputation
- ❑ Sybex's reputation
- ❑ Read book review in _____
- ❑ Other _____

6. How did you pay for this book?

- ❑ Used own funds
- ❑ Reimbursed by company
- ❑ Received book as a gift

7. What is your level of experience with the subject covered in this book?

- ❑ Beginner
- ❑ Intermediate
- ❑ Advanced

8. How long have you been using a computer?

years _____

months _____

9. Where do you most often use your computer?

- ❑ Home
- ❑ Work

- ❑ Both
- ❑ Other _____

10. What kind of computer equipment do you have? (Check all that apply)

- ❑ PC Compatible Desktop Computer
- ❑ PC Compatible Laptop Computer
- ❑ Apple/Mac Computer
- ❑ Apple/Mac Laptop Computer
- ❑ CD ROM
- ❑ Fax Modem
- ❑ Data Modem
- ❑ Scanner
- ❑ Sound Card
- ❑ Other _____

11. What other kinds of software packages do you ordinarily use?

- ❑ Accounting
- ❑ Databases
- ❑ Networks
- ❑ Apple/Mac
- ❑ Desktop Publishing
- ❑ Spreadsheets
- ❑ CAD
- ❑ Games
- ❑ Word Processing
- ❑ Communications
- ❑ Money Management
- ❑ Other _____

12. What operating systems do you ordinarily use?

- ❑ DOS
- ❑ OS/2
- ❑ Windows
- ❑ Apple/Mac
- ❑ Windows NT
- ❑ Other _____

13. On what computer-related subject(s) would you like to see more books?

_____

_____

_____

_____

14. Do you have any other comments about this book? (Please feel free to use a separate piece of paper if you need more room)

_____

_____

_____

_____

— — — — — — — — — — — — PLEASE FOLD, SEAL, AND MAIL TO SYBEX — — — — — — — — — — — — —

SYBEX INC.
Department M
2021 Challenger Drive
Alameda, CA
94501

Let us hear from you.

 Talk to SYBEX authors, editors and fellow forum members.

 Get tips, hints and advice online.

 Download magazine articles, book art, and shareware.

Join the SYBEX Forum on 🖳 **CompuServe**®

If you're already a CompuServe user, just type **GO SYBEX** to join the SYBEX Forum. If not, try CompuServe for free by calling 1-800-848-8199 and ask for Representative 560. You'll get one free month of basic service and a $15 credit for CompuServe extended services—a $23.95 value. Your personal ID number and password will be activated when you sign up.

SYBEX

Join us online today. Type **GO SYBEX** on CompuServe.
If you're not a CompuServe member, call Representative 560
at **1-800-848-8199**.

(outside U.S./Canada call 614-457-0802)